ICSEA 2024

The Nineteenth International Conference on Software Engineering Advances

September 29 - October 03, 2024

Venice, Italy

ICSEA 2024 Editors

Simona Vasilache, University of Tsukuba, Japan

Radek Kočí, Brno University of Technology, Czech Republic

Printed from e-media with permission by:

Curran Associates, Inc.
57 Morehouse Lane
Red Hook, NY 12571

Some format issues inherent in the e-media version may also appear in this print version.

International Academy, Research, and Industry Association (IARIA)
412 Derby Way
Wilmington, DE 19810

Phone: (408) 893-6407
Fax: (408) 527-6351

petre@iaria.org

Additional copies of this publication are available from:

Curran Associates, Inc.
57 Morehouse Lane
Red Hook, NY 12571 USA
Phone: 845-758-0400
Fax: 845-758-2633
Email: curran@proceedings.com
Web: www.proceedings.com

Table of Contents

ICSEA 2024

Forward

The Nineteenth International Conference on Software Engineering Advances (ICSEA 2024), held on September 29 – October 3, 2024 in Venice, Italy, continued a series of events covering a broad spectrum of software-related topics.

The conference covered fundamentals on designing, implementing, testing, validating and maintaining various kinds of software. The tracks treated the topics from theory to practice, in terms of methodologies, design, implementation, testing, use cases, tools, and lessons learnt. The conference topics covered classical and advanced methodologies, open source, agile software, as well as software deployment and software economics and education.

The conference had the following tracks:

- Advances in fundamentals for software development
- Advanced mechanisms for software development
- Advanced design tools for developing software
- Software engineering for service computing (SOA and Cloud)
- Advanced facilities for accessing software
- Software performance
- Software security, privacy, safeness
- Advances in software testing
- Specialized software advanced applications
- Web Accessibility
- Open source software
- Agile and Lean approaches in software engineering
- Software deployment and maintenance
- Software engineering techniques, metrics, and formalisms
- Software economics, adoption, and education
- Business technology
- Improving productivity in research on software engineering
- Trends and achievements

Similar to the previous edition, this event continued to be very competitive in its selection process and very well perceived by the international software engineering community. As such, it is attracting excellent contributions and active participation from all over the world. We were very pleased to receive a large amount of top quality contributions.

We take here the opportunity to warmly thank all the members of the ICSEA 2024 technical program committee as well as the numerous reviewers. The creation of such a broad and high quality conference program would not have been possible without their involvement. We also kindly thank all the authors that dedicated much of their time and efforts to contribute to the ICSEA 2024. We truly believe that thanks to all these efforts, the final conference program consists of top quality contributions.

This event could also not have been a reality without the support of many individuals, organizations and sponsors. We also gratefully thank the members of the ICSEA 2024 organizing committee for their help in handling the logistics and for their work that is making this professional meeting a success.

We hope the ICSEA 2024 was a successful international forum for the exchange of ideas and results between academia and industry and to promote further progress in software engineering research. We also hope that Venice provided a pleasant environment during the conference and everyone saved some time for exploring this beautiful city

ICSEA 2024 Steering Committee

Herwig Manaert, University of Antwerp, Belgium
Radek Koci, Brno University of Technology, Czech Republic
Sébastien Salva, University of Clermont Auvergne | LIMOS Laboratory | CNRS, France
José Carlos Metrôlho, Polytechnic Institute of Castelo Branco, Portugal
Luigi Lavazza, Università dell'Insubria – Varese, Italy
Hironori Washizaki, Waseda University / National Institute of Informatics / SYSTEM INFORMATION, Japan
Roy Oberhauser, Aalen University, Germany

ICSEA 2024 Publicity Chair

Lorena Parra Boronat, Universitat Politecnica de Valencia, Spain
Sandra Viciano Tudela, Universitat Politecnica de Valencia, Spain
Jose Miguel Jimenez, Universitat Politecnica de Valencia, Spain
Francisco Javier Díaz Blasco, Universitat Politecnica de Valencia, Spain
Ali Ahmad, Universitat Politecnica de Valencia, Spain

ICSEA 2024

Committee

ICSEA 2024 Steering Committee

Herwig Manaert, University of Antwerp, Belgium
Radek Koci, Brno University of Technology, Czech Republic
Sébastien Salva, University of Clermont Auvergne | LIMOS Laboratory | CNRS, France
José Carlos Metrôlho, Polytechnic Institute of Castelo Branco, Portugal
Luigi Lavazza, Università dell'Insubria – Varese, Italy
Hironori Washizaki, Waseda University / National Institute of Informatics / SYSTEM INFORMATION, Japan
Roy Oberhauser, Aalen University, Germany

ICSEA 2024 Publicity Chair

Lorena Parra Boronat, Universitat Politecnica de Valencia, Spain
Sandra Viciano Tudela, Universitat Politecnica de Valencia, Spain
Jose Miguel Jimenez, Universitat Politecnica de Valencia, Spain
Francisco Javier Díaz Blasco, Universitat Politecnica de Valencia, Spain
Ali Ahmad, Universitat Politecnica de Valencia, Spain

ICSEA 2024 Technical Program Committee

Tamer Abdou, Ryerson University, Canada
Morayo Adedjouma, CEA Saclay Nano-INNOV - Institut CARNOT CEA LIST, France
Abdullah Al-Alaj, Virginia Wesleyan University, USA
Ammar Kareem Obayes Alazzawi, Universiti Teknologi PETRONAS, Malaysia
Shabbab Algamdi, College of Computer Engineering and Sciences | Prince Sattam bin Abdulaziz University, Riyadh, Saudi Arabia
Washington H. C. Almeida, CESAR School, Brazil
Eman Abdullah AlOmar, Rochester Institute of Technology, USA
Sousuke Amasaki, Okayama Prefectural University, Japan
Talat Ambreen, International Islamic University, Islamabad, Pakistan
Amal Ahmed Anda, University of Ottawa, Canada
Daniel Andresen, Kansas State University, USA
Giusy Annunziata, University of Salerno, Italy
Jean-Paul Arcangeli, UPS - IRIT, France
Francesca Arcelli Fontana, University of Milano Bicocca, Italy
Oluwaseun Bamgboye, Edinburgh Napier University, Scotland
Jorge Barreiros, ISEC - Polytechnic of Coimbra / NOVA LINCS, Portugal
Marciele Bergier, Universidade do Minho | Research Center of the Justice and Governance, Portugal
Silvia Bonfanti, University of Bergamo, Italy
Mina Boström Nakicenovic, Paradox Interactive, Sweden

Khadija Bousselmi Arfaoui, University of Savoie Mont Blanc, France
José Carlos Bregieiro Ribeiro, Polytechnic Institute of Leiria, Portugal
Uwe Breitenbücher, University of Stuttgart, Germany
Antonio Brogi, University of Pisa, Italy
Carlos Henrique Cabral Duarte, Brazilian Development Bank (BNDES), Brazil
Carlos A. Casanova Pietroboni, National Technological University - Concepción del Uruguay Regional Faculty (UTN-FRCU), Argentina
Francesco Casillo, University of Salerno, Italy
Olena Chebanyuk, National Aviation University, Ukraine
Fuxiang Chen, University of Leicester, UK
Dickson Chiu, The University of Hong Kong, Hong Kong
Rebeca Cortazar, University of Deusto, Spain
André Magno Costa de Araújo, Federal University of Alagoas, Brazil
Mónica Costa, Polytechnic Institute of Castelo Branco, Portugal
Yania Crespo, University of Valladolid, Spain
Luís Cruz, Delft University of Technology, Netherlands
Beata Czarnacka-Chrobot, Warsaw School of Economics, Poland
Hepeng Dai, Chinese Aeronautical Establishment, China
Giovanni Daián Róttoli, Universidad Tecnológica Nacional (UTN-FRCU), Argentina
Darren Dalcher, Lancaster University, UK
Andrea D'Ambrogio, University of Rome Tor Vergata, Italy
Patrizio Dazzi, University of Pisa, Italy
Guglielmo De Angelis, CNR - IASI, Italy
Thiago C. de Sousa, State University of Piauí, Brazil
Maria del Carmen de Castro Cabrera, Universidad de Cádiz, Spain
Kevin Delcourt, UPS - IRIT, France
Lin Deng, Towson University, USA
Fatma Dhaou, University of Tunis el Manar, Tunisia
Dario Di Dario, University of Salerno, Italy
Jaime Díaz, Universidad de La Frontera, *Chile*
Dragos Laurentiu Dobrean, Babes-Bolyai University, Cluj Napoca, Romania
Diogo Domingues Regateiro, Instituto de Telecomunicações | Universidade de Aveiro, Portugal
Dimitris Dranidis, CITY College, University of York Europe Campus, Greece
Imke Helene Drave, RWTH Aachen University, Germany
Arpita Dutta, National University of Singapore, Singapore
Holger Eichelberger, University of Hildesheim | Software Systems Engineering, Germany
Ridha Ejbali, National Engineering School of Gabes (ENIS) / University of Gabes, Tunisia
Gledson Elias, Federal University of Paraíba (UFPB), Brazil
Fernando Escobar, University of Brasilia (UNB), Brazil
Mahdi Fahmideh, University of Southern Queensland (UniSQ), Australia
Kleinner Farias, University of Vale do Rio dos Sinos, Brazil
Thomas Fehlmann, Euro Project Office AG, Zurich, Switzerland
Alba Fernandez Izquierdo, Universidad Politécnica de Madrid, Spain
David Fernandez-Amoros, Universidad Nacional de Educación a Distancia (UNED), Spain
Estrela Ferreira Cruz, Instituto Politécnico de Viana do Castelo | ALGORIMTI research centre - Universidade do Minho, Portugal
Harald Foidl, University of Innsbruck, Austria
Stefano Forti, University of Pisa, Italy

Jonas Fritzsch, University of Stuttgart | Institute of Software Engineering, Germany
Jicheng Fu, University of Central Oklahoma, USA
Stoyan Garbatov, OutSystems SA, Portugal
Jose Garcia-Alonso, University of Extremadura, Spain
Wided Ghardallou, ENISO, Tunisia / Hail University, KSA
Gregor Grambow, Aalen University, Germany
Chunhui Guo, California State University, Los Angeles, USA
Huong Ha, University of Newcastle, Singapore
Shahliza Abd Halim, UniversityTeknologi Malaysia, Malaysia
Atsuo Hazeyama, Tokyo Gakugei University, Japan
Hussein Hazimeh, Lebanese University, Lebanon
Qiang He, Swinburne University of Technology, Australia
Jairo Hernán Aponte, Universidad Nacional de Colombia, Columbia
Bogumiła Hnatkowska, Wrocław University of Science and Technology, Poland
Syeda Sumbul Hossain, Samsung Electronics, Bangladesh
Shintaro Hosoai, Institute of Technologists, Japan
LiGuo Huang, Southern Methodist University, USA
Rui Humberto Pereira, ISCAP/IPP, Portugal
Waqar Hussain, CSIRO - Data61, Australia
Gustavo Illescas, Universidad Nacional del Centro-Tandil-Bs.As., Argentina
Irum Inayat, National University of Computer and Emerging Sciences, Islamabad, Pakistan
Florije Ismaili, South East European University, Republic of Macedonia
Angshuman Jana, IIIT Guwahati, India
Marko Jäntti, University of Eastern Finland, Finland
Judit Jász, University of Szeged, Hungary
Laid Kahloul, Biskra University, Algeria
Hermann Kaindl, Vienna University of Technology, Austria
Yasushi Kambayashi, Sanyo-Onoda City University, Japan
Ahmed Kamel, Concordia College, Moorhead, USA
Chia Hung Kao, National Taitung University, Taiwan
Dimitris Karagiannis, University of Vienna, Austria
Dimitra Karatza, iov42, UK
Vikrant Kaulgud, Accenture, India
Siffat Ullah Khan, University of Malakand, Pakistan
Radek Koci, Brno University of Technology, Czech Republic
Christian Kop, University of Klagenfurt, Austria
Blagovesta Kostova, EPFL, Switzerland
Eberhard Kranich, Euro Project Office, Duisburg, Germany
Akrivi Krouska, University of Piraeus, Greece
Bolatzhan Kumalakov, Al-Farabi Kazakh National University, Kazakhstan
Tsutomu Kumazawa, Software Research Associates Inc., Japan
Rob Kusters, Open University, The Netherlands
Alla Lake, LInfo Systems, LLC - Greenbelt, USA
Stefano Lambiase, University of Salerno, Italy
Jannik Laval, University Lumière Lyon 2 | DISP lab EA4570, Bron, France
Luigi Lavazza, Università dell'Insubria - Varese, Italy
Maurizio Leotta, University of Genova, Italy
Abderrahmane Leshob, University of Quebec at Montreal (UQAM), Canada

Mohamed Wiem Mkaouer, Rochester Institute of Technology, USA
Dietmar Winkler, Institute for Information Systems Engineering | TU Wien, Austria
Krzysztof Wnuk, Blekinge Institute of Technology, Sweden
Heitor Augustus Xavier Costa, Federal University of Lavras, Brazil
Kunpeng Xu, Université de Sherbrooke, Canada
Simon Xu, Algoma University, Canada
Rihito Yaegashi, Kagawa University, Japan
Guowei Yang, The University of Queensland, Australia
Yilong Yang, Beihang University, China
Haibo Yu, Kyushu Sangyo University, Japan
Zifan Yu, Arizona State University, USA
Mário Zenha-Rela, University of Coimbra, Portugal
Qiang Zhu, University of Michigan - Dearborn, USA
Martin Zinner, Technische Universität Dresden, Germany
Kamil Żyła, Lublin University of Technology, Poland

Copyright Information

For your reference, this is the text governing the copyright release for material published by IARIA.

The copyright release is a transfer of publication rights, which allows IARIA and its partners to drive the dissemination of the published material. This allows IARIA to give articles increased visibility via distribution, inclusion in libraries, and arrangements for submission to indexes.

I, the undersigned, declare that the article is original, and that I represent the authors of this article in the copyright release matters. If this work has been done as work-for-hire, I have obtained all necessary clearances to execute a copyright release. I hereby irrevocably transfer exclusive copyright for this material to IARIA. I give IARIA permission or reproduce the work in any media format such as, but not limited to, print, digital, or electronic. I give IARIA permission to distribute the materials without restriction to any institutions or individuals. I give IARIA permission to submit the work for inclusion in article repositories as IARIA sees fit.

I, the undersigned, declare that to the best of my knowledge, the article is does not contain libelous or otherwise unlawful contents or invading the right of privacy or infringing on a proprietary right.

Following the copyright release, any circulated version of the article must bear the copyright notice and any header and footer information that IARIA applies to the published article.

IARIA grants royalty-free permission to the authors to disseminate the work, under the above provisions, for any academic, commercial, or industrial use. IARIA grants royalty-free permission to any individuals or institutions to make the article available electronically, online, or in print.

IARIA acknowledges that rights to any algorithm, process, procedure, apparatus, or articles of manufacture remain with the authors and their employers.

I, the undersigned, understand that IARIA will not be liable, in contract, tort (including, without limitation, negligence), pre-contract or other representations (other than fraudulent misrepresentations) or otherwise in connection with the publication of my work.

Exception to the above is made for work-for-hire performed while employed by the government. In that case, copyright to the material remains with the said government. The rightful owners (authors and government entity) grant unlimited and unrestricted permission to IARIA, IARIA's contractors, and IARIA's partners to further distribute the work.

A Comparison of Closed-Source and Open-Source Code Static Measures

Luigi Lavazza
Dipartimento di Scienze Teoriche e Applicate
Università degli Studi dell'Insubria
Varese, Italy
e-mail: luigi.lavazza@uninsubria.it

***Abstract*—Most software engineering empirical studies are based on the analysis of open-source code. The reason is that open-source code is readily available, while usually software development organizations do not give access to their code, not even when the purpose is research and the code itself will not be disclosed. As a consequence, the corpus of empirical knowledge is related almost exclusively to open-source software. This poses a quite important question: do the conclusions we draw from the analysis of open-source code apply to close-source code as well? In this paper, a comparison of open-source and closed-source code is performed, to provide some preliminary answers to the question. Specifically, the goal of the paper is to evaluate whether static code measures from open-source code are similar to those obtained from close-source code. To this end, an empirical study was performed, involving closed-source code from two organizations and open-source code from a few different projects. The most popular static code measures were collected using a commercial tool, and compared. The study shows that open-source code measures appear similar to the measures obtained from industrial closed-source code. However, we must note that the study reported here involved just a few industrial projects' measures. Therefore, replications of the work presented here would be very useful.**

Keywords-software code measures; static code measures; open-source code; closed-source code.

I. INTRODUCTION

Software development organizations make their code available to researchers very rarely. This is due to their need for preserving the competitive advantage deriving from code ownership. As a consequence, the great majority of the empirical studies involving source code analyze open-source code, which is freely available. The conclusions reached by these studies are expected to apply to all code, including industrial closed-source code. However, the generalizability of studies based on open-source software relies on the assumption that closed-source software is "similar" to open-source software. Specifically, it is expected that the measures of open-source code are representative of closed-source software as well.

This paper describes an empirical study that aims at verifying if and to what extent code measures of open- and closed-source projects are similar. To this end, we measured a set of industrial closed-source projects and a set of open-source projects and compared the resulting measures.

Based on our results, there are no major differences among the measures collected from industrial and open-source projects. The study reported here has the merit to provide some initial objective evidence that studying open-source projects as representative of closed-source projects is sound.

In this study, the investigation is limited to static code measures for Java projects. Static measures can be defined at various levels of granularity (e.g., method, class, file, subsystem, etc.): here we deal only with method-level measures.

The paper is structured as follows. Section II describes the static code measures investigated in this study. Section III describes the empirical study, whose results are given in Section IV. Section V discusses the results obtained by the study. Section VI discusses the threats to the validity of the study. Section VII accounts for related work. Finally, in Section VIII some conclusions are drawn, and future work is outlined.

II. CODE MEASURES

Since the first high-level programming languages were introduced, several measures were proposed, to represent the possibly relevant characteristics of code [1]. For instance, the size of a software module is usually measured in terms of Lines Of Code (LOC), while McCabe Complexity (also known as Cyclomatic Complexity) [2] was proposed to represent the "complexity" of code, with the idea that high levels of complexity characterize code that is difficult to test and maintain. The object-oriented measures by Chidamber and Kemerer [3] were proposed to recognize poor software design. For instance, modules with high levels of coupling are supposed to be associated with difficult maintenance.

We have considered some of the most popular method-level measures used in the research literature and the software industry: they are listed in Table I.

TABLE I. THE MEASURES COLLECTED VIA SOURCEMETER.

Metric name	Abbreviation
Halstead Calculated Program Length	HCPL
Halstead Volume	HVOL
Maintainability Index (Original version)	MI
McCabe's Cyclomatic Complexity	McCC
Lines of Code	LOC

Halstead proposed several code metrics [4], based on the total number of occurrences of operators N_1, the total number of occurrences of operands N_2, the number of distinct operators η_1 and the number of distinct operands η_2. Halstead Volume (HVOL) is defined as $HVOL = (N_1 + N_2) * log_2(\eta_1 + \eta_2)$; Halstead Calculated Program Length (HCPL) is defined as $HCPL = \eta_1 * log_2(\eta_1) + \eta_2 * log_2(\eta_2)$. McCabe's complexity (McCC) is used to indicate the complexity of a program, being the number of linearly independent paths through a program's source code [2]. The Maintainability Index (MI) [5] is defined as $MI = 171 - 5.2 * ln(HVOL) - 0.23 * (McCC) - 16.2 * ln(LLOC)$, where LLOC is the number of Logical LOC, i.e., the number of non-empty and non-comment code lines.

Interested readers can find additional information concerning the definition and meaning of the selected metrics in the documentation of SourceMeter [6], the tool we used to to collect code measures.

III. The Empirical Study

The empirical study involved closed-source and open-source Java programs. This code was measured, and the collected data were analyzed via well established statistical methods. The dataset is described in Section III-A, while the measurement and analysis methods are described in Section III-B. The results we obtained are reported in Section IV.

A. The Dataset

As already mentioned, obtaining source code from software industries is not easy. Therefore, the closed-source code analyzed within the study is a convenience sample: it is the code that we were able to obtain from industrial developers. The open-source code analyzed within the study is the open-source code used within or together with the analyzed industrial projects. This guarantees a sort of "homogeneity" of code with respect to the required quality.

The projects that supplied the code for the study are listed in Table II, where some descriptive statistics are also given. Because of confidentiality reasons, the names of the industrial projects that supplied the code to be measured are not given: these projects are named Industrial1, Industrial2, Industrial3 (abbreviated Ind1, Ind2 and Ind3 where necessary). Ind1 and Ind2 are client and contract management systems from a large service company, Ind3 is the back-end of a web application. All of the industrial projects aimed to develop software supporting the main business of the owner companies, i.e., none of the considered projects delivered a product to be sold on the market. Also, all projects were developed by external software houses on behalf of the owner companies. Because of confidentiality reasons, the code and the raw measures are not available.

TABLE II. Descriptive statistics of the datasets.

	Number of files	LOC total	LOC per file mean	sd	median	range
Industrial1	1507	202299	134	268	91	[1–6851]
Industrial2	280	56419	201	286	93	[3–2336]
Industrial3	1323	250193	189	307	100	[6–3644]
Log4J	1067	126354	118	121	80	[20–1357]
JCaptcha	248	25292	102	99	75	[16–691]
Pdfbox	1215	252158	208	251	125	[21–2966]
JasperReports	3177	533008	168	285	89	[27–4398]
Hibernate	2392	236527	99	127	63	[9–2146]

Table II provides, for each analyzed project, the number of files, the total number of LOC, and the mean, standard deviation, median and range of the LOC per file.

B. The Method

The first phase of the study consisted in measuring the code. We used SourceMeter [6] to obtain the measures.

The second step consisted in selecting the data for the study. We excluded from the study all the methods having unitary McCabe complexity, i.e., the methods that contain no decision points, since those methods would bias the results. In fact, these methods are quite numerous (since they include all the setters and getters) and very small (the excluded methods have mean and median LOC in the [3,6] range).

After removing the methods having unitary McCabe complexity, we got the dataset whose descriptive statistics are given in Table III.

TABLE III. Descriptive statistics of the datasets, after removing methods with unitary McCabe complexity.

	Num. methods	LOC total	LOC per method mean	sd	median	range
Industrial1	1342	32654	24	38	15	[3,626]
Industrial2	703	17099	24	25	16	[3,197]
Industrial3	3339	127170	38	61	21	[3,1272]
Log4J	1729	29948	17	17	12	[3,176]
JCaptcha	362	6386	18	15	13	[3,100]
Pdfbox	3738	92679	25	26	16	[3,380]
JasperReports	6815	180104	26	31	17	[3,453]
Hibernate	2746	46505	17	15	12	[3,221]

The third step consisted in comparing the collected measures. To this end, we provide a visual representation of the data via boxplots that describe the distributions, the mean and the median of the measures collected from each project. We also performed statistical analysis:

1) We performed a Kruskal-Wallis test for all the considered metrics, since the conditions for performing ANOVA tests did not hold. As a result, we obtained that, for all metrics, projects are not all equivalent with respect to the considered measure.
2) To explore in detail the differences among projects, we performed Wilcoxon rank sum tests for all project pairs, for all the considered metrics.
3) When a Wilcoxon rank sum test excluded that the measures are equivalent, we evaluated the effect size via Hedge's g.

In all the performed analysis, we considered the results significant at the usual $\alpha = 0.05$ level.

IV. Results of the Study

This section reports the data collected via the empirical study, grouped according to the type of property being measured.

A. Size measures

Boxplots of LOC measures are given in Figure 1. For the sake of readability, Figure 2 provides the same data, excluding outliers. The mean values are represented as blue diamonds.

The results of the Wilcoxon rank sum tests and Hedges's g evaluations are given in Table IV. Specifically, a cell includes symbol '=' if the Wilcoxon rank sum test could not exclude that the considered measures are equivalent; otherwise, a cell includes one of the symbols 'n,' 's,' 'm' for negligible, small

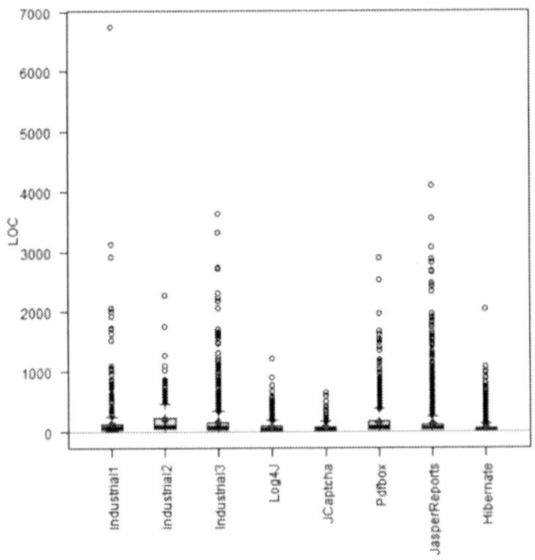

Figure 1. Boxplots of size (measured in LoC) distributions.

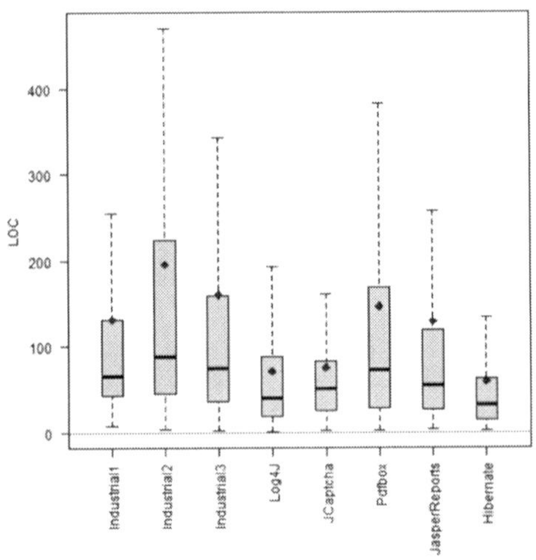

Figure 2. Boxplots of size (measured in LoC) distributions. Outliers omitted.

and medium effect size, respectively (in no case a large effect size was found).

TABLE IV. WILCOXON RANK SUM TEST AND HEDGES'S G RESULTS FOR LOC.

	Ind1	Ind2	Ind3	Log4J	JCaptcha	Pdfbox	JReports	Hibernate
Ind1	–	n	s	s	n	n	n	s
Ind2	n	–	s	s	s	=	n	s
Ind3	s	s	–	s	s	s	s	s
Log4J	s	s	s	–	n	s	s	n
JCaptcha	n	s	s	n	–	s	s	n
Pdfbox	n	=	s	s	s	–	n	s
JReports	n	n	s	s	s	n	–	s
Hibernate	s	s	s	n	n	s	s	–

B. Complexity

Boxplots of McCabe cyclomatic complexity measures are given in Figure 3. For the sake of readability, Figure 4 provides the same data, excluding outliers.

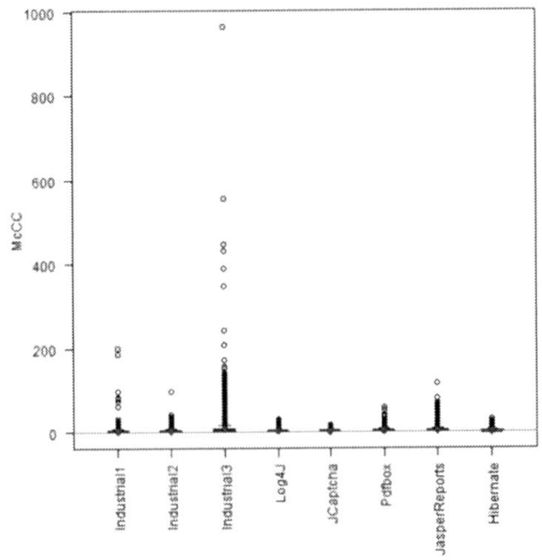

Figure 3. Boxplots of complexity (measured using McCabe cyclomatic complexity) distributions.

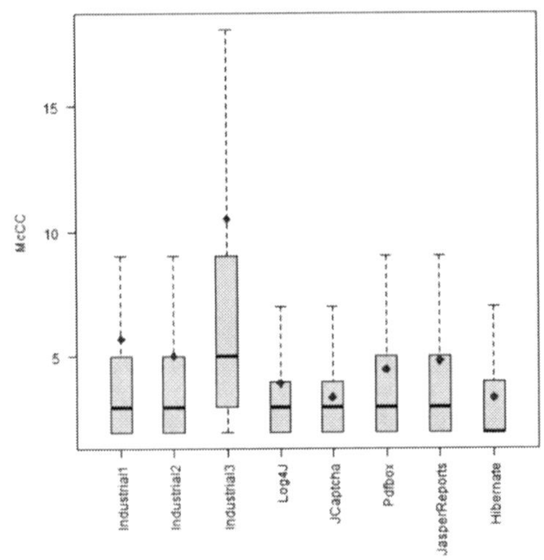

Figure 4. Boxplots of size (measured using McCabe cyclomatic complexity) distributions. Outliers omitted.

The results of the Wilcoxon rank sum tests and Hedges's g evaluations are given in Table V.

TABLE V. WILCOXON RANK SUM TEST AND HEDGES'S G RESULTS FOR MCCABE COMPLEXITY.

	Ind1	Ind2	Ind3	Log4J	JCaptcha	Pdfbox	JReports	Hibernate
Indl1	–	n	n	s	s	n	=	s
Ind2	n	–	s	s	s	=	n	s
Ind3	n	s	–	s	s	s	s	s
Log4J	s	s	s	–	n	n	n	s
JCaptcha	s	s	s	n	–	s	s	n
Pdfbox	n	=	s	n	s	–	n	s
JReports	=	n	s	n	s	n	–	s
Hibernate	s	s	s	s	n	s	s	–

C. Maintainability

Maintainability is measured via the Maintainability Index (MI) [5].

Boxplots of MI measures are given in Figure 5. For the sake of readability, Figure 6 provides the same data, excluding outliers.

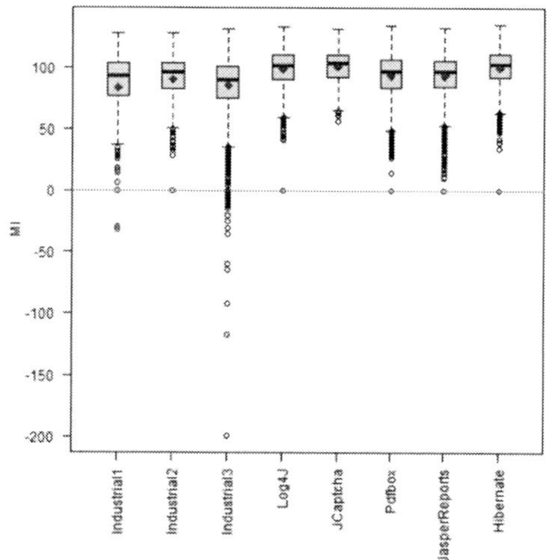

Figure 5. Boxplots of Maintainability Index MI distributions.

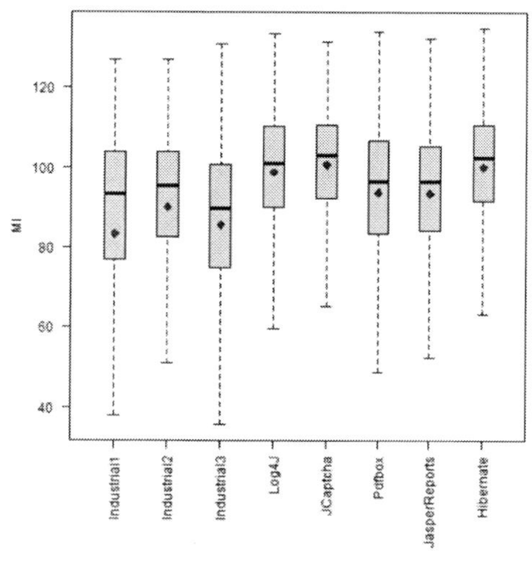

Figure 6. Boxplots of Maintainability Index MI distributions. Outliers omitted.

The results of the Wilcoxon rank sum tests and Hedges's g evaluations are given in Table VI.

TABLE VI. WILCOXON RANK SUM TEST AND HEDGES'S G RESULTS FOR THE MAINTAINABILITY INDEX (MI).

	Ind1	Ind2	Ind3	Log4J	JCaptcha	Pdfbox	JReports	Hibernate
Ind1	–	s	n	m	m	s	s	m
Ind2	s	–	n	s	m	n	n	m
Ind3	n	n	–	m	m	s	s	m
Log4J	m	s	m	–	n	s	s	n
JCaptcha	m	m	m	n	–	s	s	=
Pdfbox	s	n	s	s	s	–	n	s
JasperReports	s	n	s	s	s	n	–	s
Hibernate	m	m	m	n	=	s	s	–

D. Halstead measures

Halstead identified measurable properties of software in analogy with the measurable properties of matter [4]. Among these properties is the volume, measured via the Halstead Volume (HVOL). Boxplots of HVOL measures are given in Figure 7. For the sake of readability, Figure 8 provides the same data, excluding outliers. The results of the Wilcoxon rank sum tests and Hedges's g evaluations are given in Table VII.

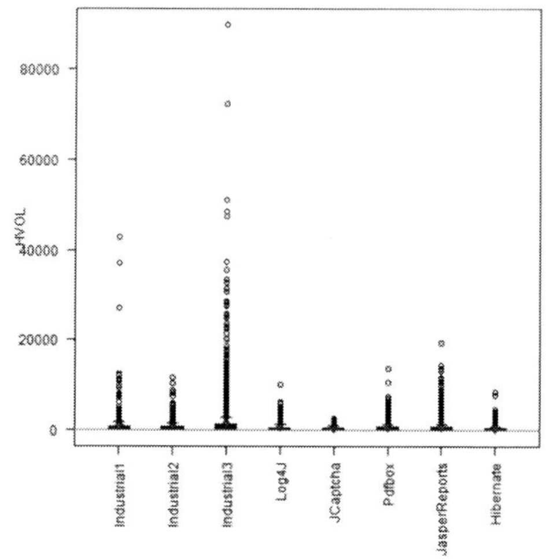

Figure 7. Halstead volume distributions.

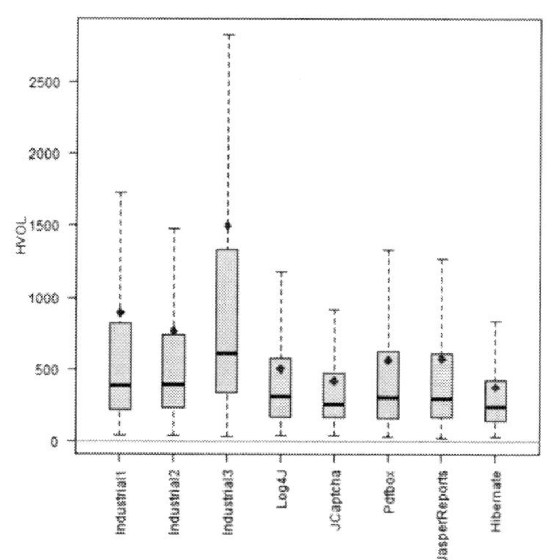

Figure 8. Halstead volume distributions. Outliers omitted.

Boxplots of Halstead Calculated Program Length (HCPL) measures are given in Figure 9. For the sake of readability, Figure 10 provides the same data, excluding outliers. The results of the Wilcoxon rank sum tests and Hedges's g evaluations are given in Table VIII.

V. DISCUSSION

Figures 1 and 2 show that the set of chosen projects are quite homogeneous with respect to size, all projects having

TABLE VII. WILCOXON RANK SUM TEST AND HEDGES'S G RESULTS FOR THE HALSTEAD VOLUME.

	Ind1	Ind2	Ind3	Log4J	JCaptcha	Pdfbox	JReports	Hibernate
Ind1	–	=	n	s	s	s	s	s
Ind2	=	–	s	s	s	s	s	m
Ind3	n	s	–	s	s	s	s	s
Log4J	s	s	s	–	n	n	=	s
JCaptcha	s	s	s	n	–	n	n	n
Pdfbox	s	s	s	n	n	–	n	s
JasperReports	s	s	s	=	n	n	–	s
Hibernate	s	m	s	s	n	s	s	–

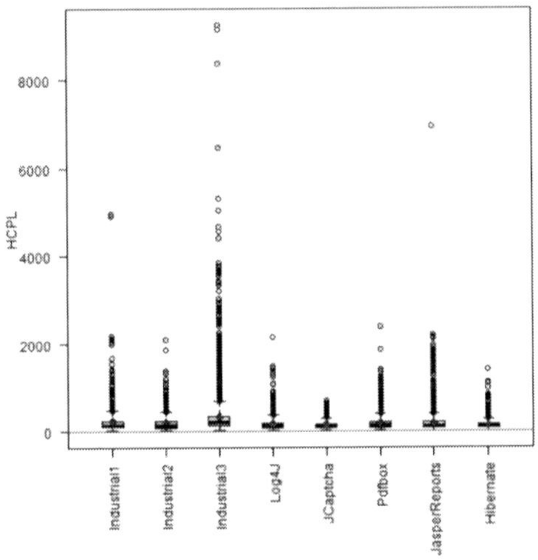

Figure 9. Halstead computed program length distributions.

the great majority of methods no longer than 200 LOC. This homogeneity is confirmed by the effect size evaluations given in Table IV: only negligible and small effect sizes were found.

Similarly, the great majority of methods have McCabe complexity not greater than 5 for all projects, with the only exception of Industrial3. However, also in project Industrial3, only outliers have alarmingly high McCabe complexity. As for LOC, the effect size is at most small, indicating substantial

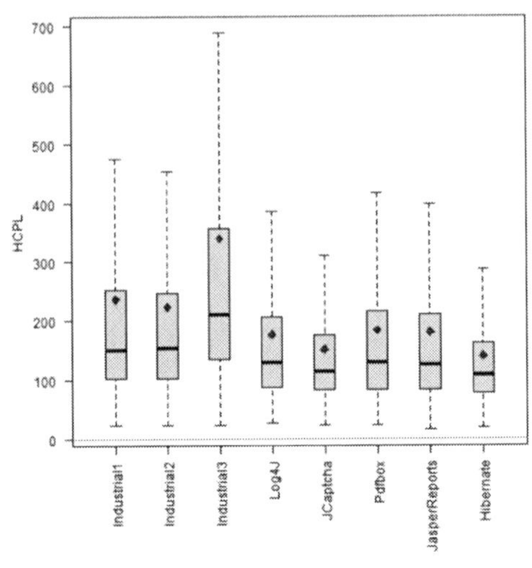

Figure 10. Halstead computed program length distributions. Outliers omitted.

TABLE VIII. WILCOXON RANK SUM TEST AND HEDGES'S G RESULTS FOR THE HALSTEAD COMPUTED PROGRAM LENGTH.

	Ind1	Ind2	Ind3	Log4J	JCaptcha	Pdfbox	JReports	Hibernate
Ind1	–	=	s	s	s	s	s	m
Ind2	=	–	s	s	s	s	s	m
Ind3	s	s	–	s	s	s	s	m
Log4J	s	s	s	–	n	=	n	s
JCaptcha	s	s	s	n	–	n	n	n
Pdfbox	s	s	s	=	n	–	n	s
JasperReports	s	s	s	n	n	n	–	s
Hibernate	m	m	m	s	n	s	s	–

equivalence of the projects' complexity measures.

Concerning the Maintainability Index, Figure 5 shows that Industrial1 and Industrial3 are the only projects that include methods with negative MI; specifically, Industrial3 has several methods with negative MI, some with alarmingly low values. So, even though the situation excluding outliers (Figure 6) seems to indicate a rather homogeneous situation, industrial projects appear to be less maintainable then open-source projects in several cases: according to Table VI, in 8 out of 15 comparisons involving a closed-source and an open-source project, the effect size was medium. Instead, comparisons involving only open-source projects and comparisons involving only closed-source projects revealed at most small effect size.

Finally, we can see that all projects are fairly homogeneous with respect to Halstead volume (Figures 7 and 8 and Table VII). Similar considerations apply for Halstead Computed Program Length (HCPL), with medium effect size differentiating industrial projects only with respect to Hibernate (Table VIII).

In conclusion, we can observe that the analyzed open-source and closed-source code appear sufficiently similar.

VI. THREATS TO VALIDITY

Concerning the application of traditional measures, we used a state-of-the-art tool (SourceMeter), which is widely used and mature, therefore we do not see any threat on this side.

A risk with the type of work presented here is that the code that companies are willing to provide to researchers might differ from the code they will not provide. This is usually due to the desire to "hide" low-quality code. In our case, it is not so: the closed-source code being measured is the complete code being used to build production applications and is representative of the companies' software in general.

Concerning the external validity of the study, as with most Software Engineering empirical studies, we cannot claim that the obtained results are generalizable. Specifically, the limited number of considered projects calls for replications of this study, involving more industrial closed-source code projects.

VII. RELATED WORK

Open-source projects have been compared with closed-source ones multiple times, but usually with respect to external perceivable qualities. In fact, many of the published papers aimed at answering questions like "Should I use this open-source software product or this closed-source one?" These papers considered issues like reliability, speed and effectiveness of defect removal, evolution, security, etc.

Bachmann and Bernstein [7] surveyed five open source projects and one closed source project to evaluate the quality and characteristics of data from bug tracking databases and version control system log files. Among other things, they discovered a poor quality in the link rate between bugs and commits.

The debate on the security of open-source software compared to that of closed-source software have produced several studies. This is due not only to the relevance of the problem, but also to the fact that security issues concerning closed-source software are publicly available, even when the source code is not.

Schryen and Kadura [8] analyzed and compared published vulnerabilities of eight open-source software and nine closed-source software packages. They provided an empirical analysis of vulnerabilities in terms of mean time between vulnerability disclosures, the development of disclosure over time, and the severity of vulnerabilities.

Schryen [9] also investigated empirically the patching behavior of software vendors/communities of widely deployed open-source and closed-source software packages. He found that it is not the particular software development style that determines patching behavior, but rather the policy of the particular software vendor.

Paulson et al. [10] compared open- and closed-source projects to investigate the hypotheses that open-source software grows more quickly, that creativity is more prevalent in open-source software, that open-source projects succeed because of their simplicity, that defects are found and fixed more rapidly in open-source projects.

As opposed to the papers mentioned above, here a fairly systematic comparison of code measures is proposed. Previously, MacCormack et al. compared the structure of an open-source system (Linux) an a closed-source system (Mozilla) [11]. With respect to our work, they evaluated just one code property (modularity) for a single pair of products.

A comparison based on code metrics involving multiple open-source and closed-source projects [12] was performed from a different point of view and using different techniques: the authors modified the Least Absolute Deviations technique where, instead of comparing metrics data to an ideal distribution, metrics from two programs are compared directly to each other via a data binning technique.

VIII. Conclusions

Open-source projects provide the code used in many empirical studies. The applicability of the results of these studies to software projects in general, i.e., including closed-source projects, is questionable, in that we are not sure that open-source code is representative of closed-source code as well.

To address this issue, in this paper, a comparison of open-source and closed-source code is performed. Specifically, static code measures from five open-source projects were compared to those obtained from three close-source projects. The study—which addressed only Java code—shows that some of the most well-known static code measures appear similar in open-source and in industrial closed-source products.

However, we recall that the study reported here involved just a few industrial projects' measures, because getting access to industrial code is not easy. Hence, the presented analysis should be regarded as a preliminary results, which needs replications before it can be considered valid in general.

Acknowledgment

The work reported here was partly supported by Fondo per la Ricerca di Ateneo, Università degli Studi dell'Insubria.

References

[1] N. Fenton and J. Bieman, *Software metrics: a rigorous and practical approach*. CRC press, 2014.

[2] T. J. McCabe, "A complexity measure", *IEEE Transactions on software Engineering*, no. 4, pp. 308–320, 1976.

[3] S. R. Chidamber and C. F. Kemerer, "A metrics suite for object oriented design", *IEEE Transactions on software engineering*, vol. 20, no. 6, pp. 476–493, 1994.

[4] M. H. Halstead, *Elements of software science*. Elsevier North-Holland, 1977.

[5] K. D. Welker, P. W. Oman, and G. G. Atkinson, "Development and application of an automated source code maintainability index", *Journal of Software Maintenance: Research and Practice*, vol. 9, no. 3, pp. 127–159, 1997.

[6] *SourceMeter*, https://www.sourcemeter.com/, [retrieved August, 2024].

[7] A. Bachmann and A. Bernstein, "Software process data quality and characteristics: A historical view on open and closed source projects", in *Proceedings of the Joint int. ERCIM workshops on Principles of software evolution (IWPSE) and software evolution (Evol) workshops*, 2009, pp. 119–128.

[8] G. Schryen, "Security of open source and closed source software: An empirical comparison of published vulnerabilities", *AMCIS 2009 Proceedings*, p. 387, 2009.

[9] G. Schryen, "A comprehensive and comparative analysis of the patching behavior of open source and closed source software vendors", in *2009 Fifth International Conference on IT Security Incident Management and IT Forensics*, IEEE, 2009, pp. 153–168.

[10] J. W. Paulson, G. Succi, and A. Eberlein, "An empirical study of open-source and closed-source software products", *IEEE transactions on software engineering*, vol. 30, no. 4, pp. 246–256, 2004.

[11] A. MacCormack, J. Rusnak, and C. Y. Baldwin, "Exploring the structure of complex software designs: An empirical study of open source and proprietary code", *Management Science*, vol. 52, no. 7, pp. 1015–1030, 2006.

[12] B. Robinson and P. Francis, "Improving industrial adoption of software engineering research: A comparison of open and closed source software", in *Proceedings of the 2010 ACM-IEEE International Symposium on Empirical Software Engineering and Measurement*, 2010, pp. 1–10.

Engineering Robotic Process Automation (RPA)

Marko Jäntti
School of Computing
University of Eastern Finland
P.O.B. 1627, Kuopio, Finland
Email: marko.jantti@uef.fi

Ville Suhonen
Digital Services, University Services
University of Eastern Finland
P.O.B 1627, Kuopio, Finland
Email: ville.suhonen@uef.fi

Maryum Hamdani
School of Computing
University of Eastern Finland
P.O.B 1627, Kuopio, Finland
Email: mhamdani@uef.fi

***Abstract*—Customer service organizations are embracing modern technologies to enhance efficiency and improve customer experiences. Software robots are playing a significant role in this transformation. This article aimed to answer the research problem: how robotic process automation (RPA) can be utilised in the automation of processes and customer service efforts? The results of the study are based on an RPA experiment carried out in Finland. Our target organization sought digitalization and automation to improve customer service processes. The main contribution of this paper is to present lessons learnt from the experiment that focused on RPA-based automation of customer service work related to the electricity interruption process. The RPA experiment was performed in collaboration with Digital Innovation Hub and an energy company in Eastern Finland in 2019.**

Keywords*—*Robotic Process Automation; software system; automation, software engineering;

I. Introduction

Robotic Process Automation (RPA) can be used for automation of routine and repeating work tasks. These work tasks may include data transfer from several data sources, such as email and spreadsheets to Enterprise Resource Planning (ERP) and Customer Relationship Management (CRM) systems [1].

RPA robots are able to read data from user interfaces of systems and can provide inputs to user interfaces in a similar way as human users could do. They also process data and communicate automatically with other systems by executing a large number of various repeating tasks enabling significant savings in working time and salary costs. A recent study [2] conducted with an auditing firm, showed that RPA can eliminate workload bottlenecks and give access to more high-quality data for auditing at low costs.

A. Background

The main purpose of using RPA is to replace human as a system user. RPA can also reduce need for expensive system improvement or system integration. Instead of implementing system improvements or performing integrations between the organization's information systems, RPA projects focus on building a robot on the top of the systems. This robot shall produce inputs to systems or read required data from systems. Therefore, there is no need to implement any changes to information systems to establish automation capabilities [3].

Software robots are used in various domains but especially financial departments and other organizations responsible for entering or processing large amounts of data have been fruitful usage targets for RPA. There are two types of robots [4]: 1) attented robots act as digital assistants for employees on their desktops and can be activated when there is a need to use them to implement a specific action, 2) unattented robots perform timed tasks independently with their own user account.

Software robots can be seen as capabilities of modern digital service management (DSM) which focuses on the exploitation of technology to manage the delivery of services consumed by customers, stakeholders, and users. IT Infrastructure Library [5] defines service management as a set of specialised organisational capabilities for enabling value for customers in the form of services. RPA may be used in all service lifecycle stages but especially on service operation [6] that involves customer service processes and large amounts of processable data.

While software robotics requires a very specific technology knowhow and advanced software engineering skills together with domain knowledge, many companies need to obtain RPA skills from outside of the organization, for example, by hiring RPA consultants or acquiring RPA implementations as a service.

B. State of the Art

RPA as a service (RPAaaS) business model enables leveraging RPA benefits and capabilities on the cloud without installing RPA software or components or purchasing specific RPA licenses [7]. One of the key benefits in using RPA is that RPA software usage is based on existing systems eliminating the need to create, replace or develop expensive platforms [8]. Yadav and Panda [9] report that organizations may struggle with making decisions on which process is to be automated or what qualities make a process ideal for automation. According to Axmann and Harmoko [10], RPA provides highest efficiency in personnel cost and requires lowest investment cost compared to other digital technologies.

Often, the items that need to be ordered for a new employee are standard as well as the operations that are performed. While this process is repeated thousands of times, this results in a large number of work hours that could be automated [11].

According to study of Ibrahim [12], automation can be divided into three types: Business Process Automation (BPR), enhanced process automation and cognitive automation. BPR contains automation of simple tasks, such as reporting. This is performed by building automatic scripts to implement tasks. Enhanced automation means automating the work activities, for example, a chat bot that answers users' questions. Cognitive automation includes learning, optimization and analytics and is used for automating more demanding tasks. By integrating AI components, deep learning and cognitive technologies to RPA, process automation becomes more intelligent and may be called 'Intelligent Process Automation' (IPA) [13].

Berruti et al. [14] have provided an alternative view of process automation stating that a complete intelligent process automation consists of five different technologies: RPA, intelligent workflows, machine learning/advanced analytics, natural language generation, and cognitive agents. In this context, intelligent workflows refer to process management software that integrates and allows monitoring of RPA processes. Ribera et al. [15] report that RPA tools are becoming increasingly intelligent with new AI-enabled features that focus on recognition, optimization, classification and extraction of knowledge from either RPA documents or processes.

This paper aims at studying automation of customer service processes through Robotic Process Automation. The remainder of the paper is organized as follows: In Section 2, research methodology of the study is presented. In Section 3, we present results of the study. Section 4 is the analysis. Finally, the conclusions are given in Section 5.

II. Research Problem & Methodology

This study aimed at answering the following research problem: how robotic process automation (RPA) can be utilised in the automation of processes and customer service efforts? In this study, we utilized an action research method to answer the research problem. The research problem was divided into following three research questions:

- How RPA-based automation is implemented in practice?
- What type of limitations or challenges are related to applying RPA?
- What measurable benefits does RPA provide?

According to Baskerville [16] action research suits particularly well studying new or changed systems development methodologies. The action research method was applied in the study because it fits well capturing and documenting change situations, such as digital transformation experiments where new technologies are used and applied to improve, automate and digitalize processes. In our study, Robotic Process Automation and related technologies represented the new systems development methodology.

A. Target Organization

Our target organization Savon Voima Oy is an energy company located in North Savo, Finland. The subsidiary Savon Voima Verkko is responsible for maintaining electricity network. Savon Voima produces and transmits both electricity and district heating. The company was interested in starting collaboration with Digital Innovation Hub and automating customer service processes with Robotic Process Automation.

B. Data Collection Methods

Data for this RPA study were collected from multiple data sources between August 2021 - May 2022 by the university research team representing the Digital Innovation Hub. The following data sources, recommended by Yin [17] and borrowed from the case study methodology, were utilized:

- Documentation: A process description and architecture description for the RPA solution related to informing customers on electricity network outages, RPA steering board memos and presentations, customer service instructions for ordering interruption cards.
- Archival records: Interruption files (csv), interruption data (xml), CRM database
- Interviews/discussions: Interviews and discussions with RPA designer, customer service and management
- Participative observation: Work meetings in target organization's facilities, a workshop on improving the communication on electricity interruptions
- Physical artifacts: a paper-based interruption card
- Direct observations: Visits to target organizations facilities, observations on customer service

Interruption files are input files that are generated by the software used for planning the electicity outages. They include name of the interruption, a list of all measurement targets that affect the interruption, start and end times for the interruption as well as the written description of the interruption. Interruption data are output files. These XML files include information on all electricity usage points and their related customers and addresses.

C. Data Analysis

Data analysis of this study was performed by case comparison technique with one unit of analysis (energy company in Finland). Case organizations were selected among industry partners of the local Digital Innovation Hub (DIH). Qualitative analysis techniques (tabularization and categorization) were used to analyze data from the different stages of the action research cycle. The research team used a research diary to capture observations during action research.

III. Results

Next the results of the case study are presented according to five steps of the action research cycle: problem identification, action planning, action taking, evaluating action and specifying learning.

A. Problem identification

The experiment started with discussion on goals and potential risks of using RPA in live production environment. The main objective of the energy company was to test RPA technology to automate the customer service process related to electricity interruptions and sending information to clients on planned interruptions. A part of this discussion is shown below:

- "Production testing of RPA should be limited and controlled. The biggest risks are situations where interruption cards are not being sent at all or some cards potentially being duplicated (if a customer service agent manually records the interruption notifications)."
- "This type of test should be carefully planned and the test results should be validated in some way."
- "For testing purposes, 100 cases will be taken from production and tested over time".
- "What are the failed cases that do not pass through RPA?
- "It is advisable to prepare the environment as an RPA user rather than in a personal role so that RPA runs can be easily performed in the future."

In the beginning of the RPA experiment, we received a document 'process and architecture description' on the target process. This included an explanation and a diagram of how the current process works at a high level. Based on the process description, we started to map out in more detail what happens in practice at different stages of the process. The process had multiple stages and its different stages were carried out by different people. These individuals were interviewed to clarify how the process works:

The process was defined as follows: In the first stage of the process in the operation center (department in the target organization), the operation engineer plans the interruption with the operation support system and forms a document called "switch field program". Information about the planned interruption is transferred to the asi battery management system. The connection program is sent by e-mail to the customer service-agent. The CSV file (interrupt file) corresponding to the switching program is stored on the network drive in a specific folder.

In the second stage of the process, the customer service representative reads the email received from the operation center and implements the corresponding entry into the CRM system. This is a manual process that reads the measurement object number from the switching program and searches the system for the planned interruption based on it. Certain actions are repeated, resulting in the interruption being stored in the system and creating an interrupt material file on the network disk containing the interruption cards. In the third stage, the interruption material is automatically transferred as an order to an external supplier to a printing service, which receives the order for the cards, prints the cards and mails them to customers.

B. Action planning

One suitable part of the entire process was selected, and automation was started. Based on the mapping of the process and preliminary information, the customer service representative's "order interrupt cards" phase was confirmed as the most suitable part.

This part of the process mainly involves manual data entry into the system and is therefore well suited for automation.In addition, another part of the process was raised, the improvement of which and the possibilities of automation could be considered. At the moment, a small number of customers are involved in electronic outage communications, and the aim was to explore different possibilities for advertising the electronic service to customers.

The required interface functionalities were not available for the part of the process selected for automation, so automation should be implemented with robotic process automation through a user interface. The aim would therefore be to implement a program that can be scheduled to read new interrupt files from a network drive and, based on them, create an interrupt in the CRM system, just as a customer service representative would do it through the user interface.

In the organization's upcoming RPA project, various software solutions for RPA implementation and process automation were tested. The options considered were Python, UiPath, SSIS, Automation Anywhere, WorkFusion, and Kofax. However, the researcher was given the freedom to implement the process using their preferred tool. In practice, this meant either an open-source Python implementation or UiPath, as it is free and readily available, and no procurement decision had been made for any other software. The study decided to explore available Python libraries since Python was already a familiar tool for the researcher, and they also wanted to determine whether such automations could be realistically implemented using open-source software.

The chosen Python library for use is called "pywinauto." The organization was also interested in testing this library. With pywinauto, it is possible to automate the usage of Windows program interfaces, bringing typical RPA functionalities to Python12. Currently, it is one of the most popular open-source options for this purpose. Among the free options for desktop automation, other popular choices include PyAutoGUI, which allows control of keyboard and mouse inputs1, Sikuli(X), based on image recognition2, and AutoHotkey, which focuses more on scripting keyboard shortcuts3. Python also has a Selenium WebDriver implementation that enables web browser automation.

C. Action taking

Pywinauto utilizes Microsoft's UI Automation (UIA) interface for user interface automation. Through this interface, software can read information about UI elements and provide input to the user interface. It can be used for automating interfaces or for automated testing of interfaces. UIA represents all UI elements as objects in a tree structure, showing their relationships to each other. The root node of the tree corresponds to the desktop

In practice, automation with Pywinauto involves locating an element in the tree, writing code to reference it appropriately, and performing the desired action. Most often, elements are referenced as child windows of another element, and the actions typically involve mouse clicks. Elements can be referenced by name, automation ID, or class name. Information about the elements of an executable program can be explored using various tools, with Microsoft's Inspect tool being one of the commonly used options.

In addition to clicking or activating different elements, it's also possible to control user interfaces directly by sending keyboard commands. This can speed up the execution of processes by avoiding the programmatic search for elements within complex UI structures. For example, using keyboard shortcuts in applications is even recommended, as they usually remain consistent even when the UI changes due to updates. Occasionally, keyboard-based control may be necessary if other solutions for navigation are not available.

Pywinauto is built as an object-based automation tool, but in practice, at least during the research, it wasn't possible to reference the elements as cleanly as intended in the context of an automated application.The implemented robot aims to mimic the process performed by a customer service agent as accurately as possible. While a customer service agent receives assignments via email, the robot retrieves them directly from the network drive. This approach is simpler than reading emails programmatically. Additionally, it reduces the workload on the sender's side, which is the service center.

The robot monitors a specific directory on the network drive where interruption plans created by the service center arrive in .csv format. Such an interruption file contains information about all measurement points affected by the interruption. The robot extracts one measurement point identifier from this file and stores it in a variable. Using this identifier, it retrieves all interruptions related to that measurement point, selects the appropriate interruption, and extracts a unique name created for that interruption. This name is then used to retrieve the locations and customers affected by the interruption during its creation.

Creating an interruption concludes with ordering interruption cards. In this step, the robot selects all rows (i.e., customers) affected by the interruption and clicks the 'Print Interruption Cards' button. This generates the 'interruption material,' an .xml file placed in a specific directory. The file contains information about all customers previously selected from the user interface, formatted in a specific way. Based on the location number, the robot extracts customers' names and postal addresses to which the interruption cards will be delivered.

From this directory, the file is forwarded to an external printing and mailing service. This external entity prints the cards using the provided data and handles their delivery to the customers. If the robot encounters an error and cannot complete the process, it logs this information and sends a notification about the incomplete interruption to the customer service email. The same interruption is not retried; any problematic cases are manually addressed as usual. The interruption process with and without RPA is presented in Fig. 1.

For the purpose of implementation testing, a small-scale test plan was created. The testing was carried out in a test environment that closely resembles the production environment. One hundred old interruption files were copied from the production environment to the test environment. This was considered a sufficient quantity for fairly comprehensive testing. The process was executed on the imported interruptions in the test environment in the same way it would operate in the actual production environment.

The resulting XML-formatted interruption data was compared to the original interruption data generated by the current process. For this purpose, a script was written to read both

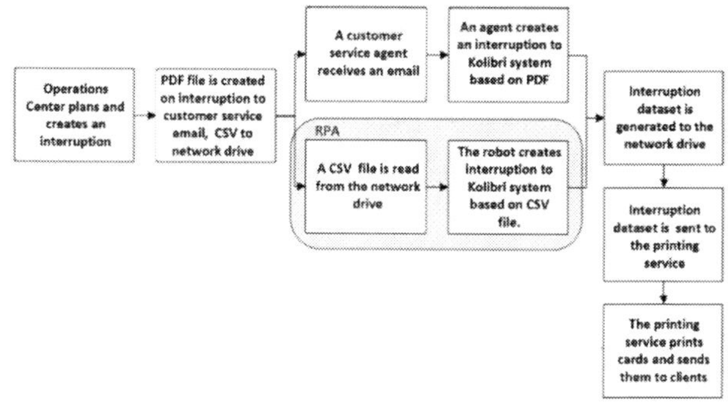

Fig. 1. The interruption process (RPA vs. traditional)

XML files and ensure they contain the same content. While the order of items in the output files may differ, the content should remain consistent. During testing, several issues were identified and corrected. The testing process also revealed various exceptional cases, necessitating the development of handling logic.

Another part of the process, which was considered somewhat separate from the actual RPA implementation during the study, related to improving customer communication. An employee of Savon Voima stated that informing customers about planned power outages using paper-based interruption cards (see Fig. 2.) costed Savon Voima an estimated 100Keur annually.

To achieve smoother communication and potential cost savings, the goal is to transition all customers to electronic communication. The organization already had a mobile application for this purpose, but naturally, not all customers used this alternative communication channel. To enable the adoption of electronic interruption communication, customers need to download the application from the app store and register as users. In 2021, Savon Voima switched to electronic communications (push notification to the Väppi mobile application, SMS and email).

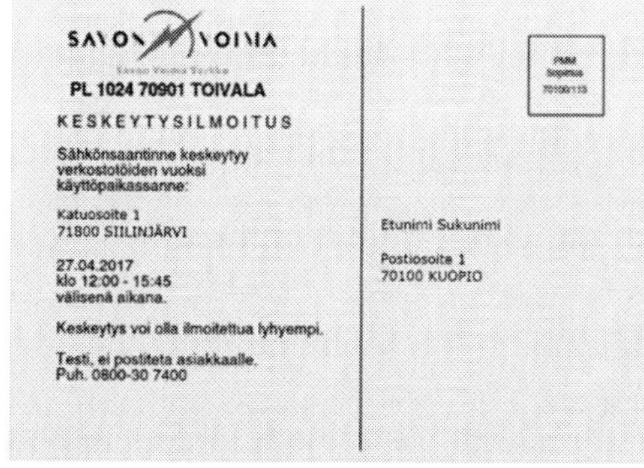

Fig. 2. The interruption card that is sent to the electricity company's customers

As part of the study, a workshop was organized to discuss improvements in customer communication. Key observations from the workshop included the possibility of promoting the mobile application on the existing paper interruption cards.

To facilitate app download and adoption, a QR code could be used, directing customers seamlessly to the app store via an information page. During the workshop, practical usability testing of the mobile application and the implementation of disruption notifications were also conducted. The tester identified areas for improvement in the adoption process and the application's user interface, which were documented and discussed during the workshop. One of the improvement areas was to highlight the option for subscribing to disruption notifications within the app.

Previously, the organization had proposed implementing a text message campaign related to disruptions. This would involve identifying customers who do not yet subscribe to electronic messages during the disruption creation process and sending them promotional texts about the service. However, this implementation would have required information about which customers associated with the disruption were already engaged with electronic communication. Obtaining this data would have been possible only from the mobile app provider's database, but no interface was developed for this purpose, so the project has not yet been realized.

D. Evaluating the action

The currently manual process is estimated to take approximately 4 minutes when performed by a customer service representative. In 2018, the process was repeated 1251 times, resulting in a total execution time of 83 hours per year. Since the entire process can be automated by a robot, this would save 83 hours of working time annually, which could be allocated to more meaningful tasks. With an average mothly salary 3500 eur (hourly salary 21,88 eur), this would result in 1816 eur direct annual savings.

Significantly bigger costs savings can be achieved by guiding customers to select a digital channel for receiving information on electricity outages which would decrease costs related to printing paper-based interruption cards. Unfortunately, due to the constraints of the study, a formal evaluation of the implementation's performance in production was not conducted. The software robot had difficulties to open some complicated UI elements but it worked surprisingly well as whole. Regarding scalability, as more automated processes start to accumulate, monitoring and managing them becomes difficult without dedicated tools.

As a result of the project, the organization obtained the initial version of the RPA implementation. The focus of this implementation was automating a specific application used by the organization using the pywinauto library. Additionally, the insights gained from this project may partially inform future solutions involving other processes that utilize the same software. In 2024, one of the directors of Savon Voima commented: "RPA pilot carried out in 2019 has contributed partly to the RPA development of our organization. Today, there are a total of 450 connections between information systems, which do not necessarily only transfer data, in production."

E. Specifying learning

An end-to-end automation of a single process was implemented for the organization as part of a broader RPA project. At times, different stakeholders struggled to grasp the core idea of what they were actually doing. Similar to the previous case, not everyone shared the same understanding of various terms. For many, comprehending the concept of a software robot and its role can be challenging.

TABLE I. ANALYSIS OF ACTION RESEARCH STUDY

Research question	Finding	Category
RQ1	Focus on interruptions	Well-defined scope
RQ1	Carefull assessment of automation target	Planning automation
RQ1	Pywinauto and Microsoft UI Automation	RPA technologies
RQ1	Jenkins for RPA management	RPA management
RQ2	Need for dedicated mgmt tools	RPA management
RQ2	Errors due to misreading UI	Complex UI
RQ2	Small RPA team	Limited RPA resources
RQ2	RPA terminology is difficult	Communication
RQ3	Annual salary savings 1816 eur	Decreased costs
RQ3	Decreased printing costs	Decreased costs
RQ3	86 h time savings annually	Time savings
RQ3	Identification of other improv.	Impr. ideas
RQ3	Increased RPA knowhow inhouse	Skills improvement

At some point, there was even debate about whether this was truly an RPA solution or simply system integration. During the study, we learned the importance of accurately understanding and documenting the process from the outset. Several exceptional cases emerged during development that could have been addressed more effectively if they had been included in the initial process description. Precise and accurate process documentation and flowcharts are crucial documents for seamless automation. Effective communication with the customer is also essential.

The project was largely conducted remotely, which posed communication challenges. Relying solely on email communication can slow down the process, as immediate clarification on process details may not always be possible. When implementing RPA with an external partner, consider using alternative communication channels such as Microsoft Teams instead of relying solely on email. Pywinauto appears to be one of the few comprehensive Python libraries for Windows GUI automation. While the underlying idea of the software seems promising, its usage can be quite challenging, especially in the early stages. Working with Pywinauto is less intuitive compared to tools like UiPath.

IV. ANALYSIS

In Table 1, analysis of action research study results reflecting the three research questions (RQ1: RPA implementation, RQ2: Limitations/challenges of RPA, RQ3: Benefits of RPA) of the study is presented.

The selection of processes for automation is a crucial part of process automation. Not all processes can be automated immediately. Often, processes believed to yield the most savings through automation are prioritized for implementation. Extremely complex processes should also not be the first candidates for automation, if at all. At Savon Voima, processes were carefully assessed and prioritized for automation. The goal was to initially automate time-consuming, frequently repetitive manual processes. Savon Voima specifically embraced RPA (Robotic Process Automation) for their process automation efforts.

Savon Voima considered Python-based implementations as well. Python has indeed become a significant tool, especially in the field of data science, and it's well-suited for various automation tasks. Ultimately, the project was implemented using Python. Based on this experiment, both UiPath and Python appear to be intriguing and popular solutions for automation. While UiPath stands out as a well-known RPA tool, Python's versatility and widespread adoption make it a powerful choice for automation as well.

In addition to technical challenges, organizations may encounter difficulties during process adoption. When implementing a new process, it's crucial to adequately inform and guide all personnel involved. Unfortunately, Savon Voima's project didn't progress to the production phase, so formal communication didn't occur during the project. However, the staff received information about the RPA project and participated in demos. Effective communication is essential in automation projects. Within the organization, there seemed to be uncertainty about the meanings of terms, such as RPA and artificial intelligence (AI).

V. Conclusion

This study aimed at answering the research problem: How robotic process automation (RPA) can be utilised in the automation of processes and customer service efforts? The main contribution of this paper is to present lessons learnt from an Robotic Process Automation experiment concerning planned electricity outages and related customer service process.

There were three research questions in the study. Regarding the first research question, we made many useful observations how RPA-based automation is implemented in practice? Our solution was based on Pywinauto that uses Microsoft UI Automation (UIA) interface in automating the user interface behavior. Through this interface, the software is able to read information about the elements of the user interface, as well as provide input to the user interface. We observed that it could be also possible to combine a machine learning module, such as MS Cognitive services, with an automation process.

Concerning the second research question, what type of limitations or challenges are related to applying RPA, we identified potential scalability challenges. While more automated processes start to accumulate, monitoring and managing them becomes difficult without dedicated management tools. This shall very likely increase the costs of RPA implementation. Additionally, we observed that the software robot could not reach some UI elements.

Finally, related to the third research question, we studied measurable benefits that RPA can provide. We found that our RPA system could result in 83 hours annual savings in work hours meaning 1816 eur direct annual savings (calculated with 3500 eur salary costs) in the scenario that we selected. However, during our RPA experiment, we also found improvement potential in digital channels that enable receiving information on interruptions.

There are certain limitations related to the action research method. First, the results of the study might be difficult to generalize to other organisations because the business context, technologies, service processes, communication ways on interruptions, digital channels in receiving information on interruptions may vary significantly between organizations. Second, due to limited time available for implementation we could not reach the statys of an operational service. Third, more employees could have been interviewed to identify additional use cases for RPA. Further research could focus on studying Intelligent Process Automation for automating service processes.

Acknowledgment

We would like to thank Savon Voima for valuable collaboration during the study. The RPA experiment was conducted as part of Digiteknologian TKI-ympäristö (Digikeskus) project (ERDF, North Savo Regional Council, A74338)

References

[1] S. Aguirre and A. Rodriguez, "Automation of a business process using robotic process automation (rpa): A case study," in *Communications in Computer and Information Science - Applied Computer Sciences in Engineering*. Cham, Switzerland: Springer International Publishing, 2017, pp. 65–71.

[2] A. S. Tømmervåg, T. Bach, and B. Jæger, "Leveraging the competition: Robotic process automation (rpa) enabling competitive small and medium sized auditing firms," in *2022 IEEE/SICE International Symposium on System Integration (SII)*, 2022, pp. 833–837.

[3] W. Aalst, M. Bichler, and A. Heinzl, "Robotic process automation," *Business & Information Systems Engineering*, vol. 60, 05 2018.

[4] P. Lewicki, J. Tochowicz, and J. van Genuchten, "Are robots taking our jobs? a roboplatform at a bank," *IEEE Software*, vol. 36, no. 3, pp. 101–104, 2019.

[5] Axelos, *ITIL Foundation - ITIL 4 Edition*. Stationary Office Books, UK, 2019.

[6] C. Office, *ITIL Service Operation*. The Stationary Office, UK, 2011.

[7] C. Dilmegani, "The ultimate guide to rpa as a service (rpaas) in 2024," https://research.aimultiple.com/rpa-as-a-service/, January 2024.

[8] J. G. Enríquez, A. Jiménez-Ramírez, F. J. Domínguez-Mayo, and J. A. García-García, "Robotic process automation: A scientific and industrial systematic mapping study," *IEEE Access*, vol. 8, pp. 39 113–39 129, 2020.

[9] N. Yadav and S. Panda, "A path forward for automation in robotic process automation projects: Potential process selection strategies," in *2022 International Conference on Machine Learning, Big Data, Cloud and Parallel Computing (COM-IT-CON)*, vol. 1, 2022, pp. 801–805.

[10] B. Axmann and H. Harmoko, "Robotic process automation: An overview and comparison to other technology in industry 4.0," in *2020 10th International Conference on Advanced Computer Information Technologies (ACIT)*, 2020, pp. 559–562.

[11] L. P. Willcocks, M. C. Lacity, and A. Craig, "The it function and robotic process automation," *LSE Research Online Documents on Economics*, 2015.

[12] A. Ibrahim and S. Abd-elrehim, "A study about using a cognitive agent in replacing level 1 and 2 service desk activities"."

[13] P. S. Kholiya, A. Kapoor, M. Rana, and M. Bhushan, "Intelligent process automation: The future of digital transformation," in *2021 10th International Conference on System Modeling & Advancement in Research Trends (SMART)*, 2021, pp. 185–190.

[14] F. Berruti, G. Nixon, G. Taglioni, and R. Whiteman, "Intelligent process automation: The engine at the core of the next-generation operating model," *McKinsey Digital*, 3 2017.

[15] J. Ribeiro, R. Lima, T. Eckhardt, and S. Paiva, "Robotic process automation and artificial intelligence in industry 4.0 – a literature review," *Procedia Computer Science*, vol. 181, pp. 51–58, 2021.

[16] R. Baskerville, "Investigating information systems with action research," *Commun. AIS*, p. 4.

[17] R. Yin, *Case Study Research: Design and Methods, Fourth edition*. Beverly Hills, CA: Sage Publishing, 2009.

Assessing Usability Attributes and Metrics: Causes and Causalities in SCADA Systems for the Forestry Industry

Eino Haikonen
Department of Computing
University of Turku
Turku, Finland
email: eino.a.haikonen@utu.fi

Anne-Maarit Majanoja
Department of Computing
University of Turku
Turku, Finland
email: anne-maarit.majanoja@utu.fi

***Abstract*—As operations and systems become more complex, usability and user experience become increasingly critical. Organizations invest significant resources to enhance usability, yet identifying context-dependent root causes remains challenging. This paper describes a usability study conducted by a Finnish forestry company on a Supervisory Control And Data Acquisition (SCADA) control system. The study utilized academic research to identify key usability attributes and metrics, which formed the basis of a comprehensive usability questionnaire. Analysis of survey responses underscores the importance of situational analysis and identifying cumulative and causal influences on end-user perceptions of usability.**

***Index Terms*—Usability; User Experience (UX); Industry survey; Usability metrics and attributes; SCADA Control/supervisory system; Root-cause; Causality**

I. Introduction

As information technology becomes more widespread, designing IT devices, applications, and systems to best serve end-users has become crucial. This is particularly evident in industry, where technological progress drives development and introduces new technologies into production [1]. However, these advances increase system complexity, adding features, functionalities, and data [2]. Consequently, as systems become more complex, their perceived usability declines, challenging the implementation of user-friendly interfaces [3] [2].

The goal of user interface design is to develop usability-focused interfaces. Usability refers to practical aspects that make a system easy to use, while user experience (UX) encompasses the broader, holistic experience of using the system [4] [5]. Software engineering defines usability through various attributes, with frameworks and measures provided by the International Organization for Standardization (ISO) in standards like ISO 9241 and ISO/IEC 25000:2014 [6] [7]. The challenge lies in finding metrics appropriate to the organization's context.

Organizations invest significant time and resources in improving system usability and need end-user feedback to make improvements. However, exhaustive surveys often fail to produce clear, measurable results. Instead, time and effort should be spent designing the survey and defining appropriate metrics. This is where academic research proves valuable. By aligning industry needs with academic methodologies, new capabilities and insights can be developed for the industry.

This paper describes how a Finnish forestry company evaluated the usability of its Supervisory Control And Data Acquisition (SCADA) system. The study, conducted in collaboration with the company, focused on the experiences of operators using the SCADA system. The purpose of this study was to evaluate the usability of the SCADA system and identify areas for improvement through an understanding of the root causes of usability issues. This paper addresses the RQ: How to measure SCADA system usability to better understand underlying usability challenges and enhance system usability development? First, academic research identified key usability attributes and metrics to assess the current state of the operational SCADA system. Second, an end-user survey was designed and deployed, with questions linked to these specific usability attributes. Third, the survey results were analyzed to uncover root causes and causalities behind the responses and end-user experiences.

This paper is structured as follows. In Section II, we present the results of the literature review. Section III presents the SCADA system that the forestry company wants to evaluate. In Section IV, we define the usability attributes that will be used to conduct the survey. In Section, V we present the results of the survey and analyse the survey responses. In Section VI, we discuss the findings of the study, the cause-effect relationships and the related causalities and cumulative effects. And finally, in Section VII the conclusion of the study.

II. Literature review

This literature review explores the existing research on defining and measuring usability attributes and metrics, focusing on their application to user interface design. The following search terms: "usability attributes," "user interface," "attributes," and "metrics," were used in the ACM Digital Library database to identify recent studies. The selection criteria included articles written in English, scientific in nature (excluding dissertations), related to usability metrics/attributes and user interfaces (excluding mobile usability), published between 2004-2024, and containing the search terms in the title. Initially, 35 articles were identified, which were then narrowed down to nine (article id: [8]–[16]) based on their relevance to the topic, assessed through a review of their titles, abstracts, and finally, the full articles. Where appropriate, the literature search was supplemented with usability-related standards, such as ISO standards, and well-known usability frameworks, such as the Nielsen's Usability Framework [17].

Definitions and Standards. Usability and user experience (UX) are fundamental concepts in human-computer interaction. Usability focuses on practical aspects like efficiency, effectiveness, and satisfaction, making a system easy to use. In contrast, UX encompasses the broader, holistic experience, including emotions, attitudes, and overall satisfaction. Although distinct, usability and UX are closely related and complementary, collectively defining how well a system meets user needs and expectations [4]. Several standards have defined and described usability attributes, with the International Organization for Standardization (ISO) being particularly notable. ISO 9241-11 defines usability in terms of effectiveness, efficiency, and satisfaction [6]. This standard was later expanded to include additional measures specific to computer software usability, as described in ISO/IEC 25023:2016 ([18]. These measures include appropriateness recognizability, learnability, operability, user error protection, user interface aesthetics, and accessibility [19]. The ISO 9126 standard [20] (now revised as ISO/IEC 25010:2023 [21]) also includes attributes such as learnability, operability, and accessibility. These standards provide a comprehensive framework for evaluating and improving usability across various systems and applications.

Measurement Approach. Previous research highlights various approaches to measuring usability. The concept of user experience (UX) has been introduced to take into account the emotions and attitudes of the user when using a particular product, system or service [22] [23]. Nielsen's usability model [24] [17] includes attributes such as learnability, efficiency, memorability, errors, and satisfaction [17] [25]. Learnability refers to how easy a system is to learn. Efficiency refers to system usage effectiveness. Memorability refers to how easy the system is to use and remember after having used it. Errors refers to the number of errors in using the system, the system's ability to recover from errors, and the potential for serious errors in using the system. Satisfaction refers to how pleasant the system is to use [24] [26]. These attributes provide a comprehensive framework and attributes for evaluating the usability of a system.

Application of Usability Measures Across Different Domains. Previous studies have effectively applied usability measures to specific domains such as e-learning [14] and e-commerce [15], demonstrating the versatility and adaptability of these metrics. In the context of e-learning systems, usability attributes have been assessed through user surveys to measure success and identify areas for improvement [14]. Similarly, in the domain of e-commerce, researchers have identified key factors that affect website usability and examined how these factors enhance user effectiveness and satisfaction [15]. Furthermore, previous studies have proposed various evaluation measures to assess specific elements of usability. For instance, the layout of a user interface can be evaluated to ensure clarity and ease of use [10]. Additionally, standards such as ISO 25010 have been utilized to transform quality models into explicit and interpretable measurement tools, providing a structured approach to evaluating and improving usability [16]. These examples highlight the broad applicability of usability metrics across different fields and the importance of using standardized measures to achieve consistent and reliable results.

Intuitiveness and Industry 4.0 Expectations in System Usability. Usability is significantly influenced by the intuitiveness of the system. The intuitive nature of a system is rooted in the user's prior experiences with similar systems, which makes an intuitive system easier to learn and use. This familiarity facilitates the quick adoption and efficient use of new systems [26]. Industry 4.0 expectations for system interfaces were also taken into account. These expectations include providing an up-to-date description of the system state, timely responses to changes in the system state, and clear, understandable notifications or messages to users about the system state. These features are designed to assist users in making informed decisions across various situations where the system requires them to react or take action [2].

The Gap between Academic Research and Industry in Usability. One of the major goals and challenges in software engineering is to bridge the gap between effective academic research and industry practice to create a meaningful impact on the industry [12]. Based on previous research, a common approach to evaluating usability involves asking participants to perform specific tasks and answer detailed questions about their characteristics, preferences, experiences, and learning. This method helps identify a set of categories and usability attributes to consider [8]. Measuring usability is widely recognized as one of the most challenging tasks for system development teams. Consequently, previous studies have identified usability attributes from existing usability models, incorporating insights from both practitioners and researchers [13]. Previous research has highlighted several key issues, including the limited focus on real business problems and the disconnect between research and practical application [9]. This disconnect often results in research that is not rooted in real-world settings, making the findings less applicable and scalable. To address these challenges, it is essential to develop context-driven research [11]. Such research should be grounded in the actual needs of each specific domain to ensure that the results are relevant, actionable, and capable of making a significant impact. This literature review informs the usability survey design, with details on the survey implementation and attributes discussed in Section IV.

III. Introduction to SCADA System

SCADA is a system used to control and monitor industrial applications [28]. Key features of SCADA systems are to

TABLE I
USABILITY ATTRIBUTES AND METRICS IDENTIFIED TO EVALUATE THE USABILITY OF THE SCADA SYSTEM

	Attribute/metric	Description	Reference
1.	Effectiviness (ISO)	Achieved targets, performed tasks, errors in task performance, intensity of errors	[24], [27]
2.	Efficiency (ISO and Nielsen)	Time spent on the task, time efficiency, redundant activities	[24], [26] [6] [27]
3.	Satisfaction (ISO and Nielsen)	Overall satisfaction, satisfaction with features, use of features, user confidence, perceived comfort and convenience	[24], [26] [6], [27]
4.	Learnability (ISO ja Nielsen)	Simplicity of the system, time, completeness of instructions, default values for input fields, understandability of error messages, understandability of user interface	[24], [26]
5.	Memorability (Nielsen)	Ease of use, memorability after a break in use	[24], [26]
6.	Errors/User error protection (ISO and Nielsen)	Number of errors, recovery from errors, impact of errors	[24], [26] [19]
7.	Appropriateness recognisability (ISO)	Fitness for purpose	[19]
8.	Operability (ISO)	Consistency of functionality and layout, clarity of messages, customisability of functionalities and user interface, auditability, cancellation of actions, understandable categorisation of information	[19]
9.	User interface aesthetics (ISO)	Aesthetic satisfaction	[19]
10.	Accessability (ISO)	Accessibility for disabled users, supported languages	[19]
11.	Up-to-date information (Industry 4.0 user inferfaces)	Up-to-date representation of the process status	[2]
12.	Supporting the user in decision making (Industry 4.0 user interfaces)	Providing the necessary information to support the user's decision making	[2]
13.	Intuitivity	Intuitive to use	[26]

visualize physical production processes through the system, communicate information related to the production process, and remote control equipment related to the production process. SCADA systems are Cyber-Physical Systems (CPS). They connect physical devices, machines, and IT systems related to the production process into a coherent entity via a data network [29]. This integration enables real-time production data acquisition, data processing and transmission, and process management through a single interface. SCADA also enables fully automated controls that dynamically respond to the production process. [30] In the context of this paper, a SCADA system at a forestry company's production plant is responsible for controlling almost the entire production process of the plant. The primary control of the process is centralized in the plant's central control room but several SCADA interfaces are also located at the plant's physical production facilities. The SCADA interface is a traditional graphical user interface (GUI), keyboard and mouse. Interfaces located on the production floor have also touch screens. The forest company's production facility is divided into five departments and each department has a unique SCADA view(s).

IV. INDUSTRY SURVEY IMPLEMENTATION: DEFINING USABILITY ATTRIBUTES AND EXECUTING THE SURVEY

Conducting the study involved four main steps: 1) identifying usability attributes based on academic research and standards, 2) defining a usability survey based on these attributes, 3) conducting the survey within the company, and 4) analyzing the survey results (in Sections V and VI).

The first and most critical step was to compile the usability attributes to be evaluated during the study. The company recognized that a focused effort was needed to select the attributes that would best serve its objectives. This required familiarity with usability research and a combination of academic and business needs and insights. Based on the usability definitions presented in Section II, the study identified the following usability attributes to be used to evaluate the SCADA system (Table I):

- ISO 9241 and Nielsen: Effectiveness, Efficiency, Satisfaction, Learnability, and Memorability [6] [27] [24] [26]
- ISO 25023 and Karnouskos: Errors/User error protection, Appropriateness recignisability, Operability, User interface aesthetics, Accessability [18] [19]
- Industry 4.0 user interfaces: Up-to-date information and Supporting the user in decision making [2]
- Intuitivity [26]

The second step of usability research was to define the survey. Table I lists the usability attributes, their sources, descriptions and references. Based on this table, the questionnaire was designed and structured to ensure that each question corresponded to a specific usability attribute. The questionnaire consisted of 13 statements derived from the usability attributes and metrics, as well as the practical experience with the SCADA system in the forestry company.

The first-hand work experience of one of the authors with the use of the SCADA system in the forestry company was also used to define the statements. All statements in the questionnaire were closed-ended, 7-point yes/no Likert scale questions. Using a 7-point Likert Scale was chosen to provide more variation in the results of the questionnaire, thus providing more accurate results. In the questionnaire, a Likert scale of 1 indicates that the respondent strongly disagrees with the statement and 7 indicates that the respondent strongly agrees with the statement (Figure 1). For question 11, the

Likert scale was reversed and is therefore shown separately from the other questions (Figure 2). All questions in the questionnaire were mandatory. Open-ended questions at the end of the survey enabled participants to clarify their answers and provide additional comments on SCADA usability. Personal and background information of the users was fully anonymized. The survey only required respondents to specify their department within the plant and their SCADA experience duration (more or less than one year).

The third step was to collect the survey responses. The data collection process for the SCADA usability case study was conducted as an electronic Webropol-survey between 14.2.2023-11.1.2024. The questionnaire was open for voluntary participation by operators using SCADA in their operations. The questionnaire was sent out to a limited number of operators by a manager of the forestry company. This limited the number of potential respondents, but also improved the value and quality of the responses received.The questionnaire and the instructions on how to complete the survey were distributed to the operators in the forest enterprise through the internal communication channels.

V. Results of the Survey

The fourth and most significant step of the study was analyzing the results and identifying root causes and causality (in Section VI). All departments within the plant participated in the survey, resulting in a total of 19 responses on SCADA usability.

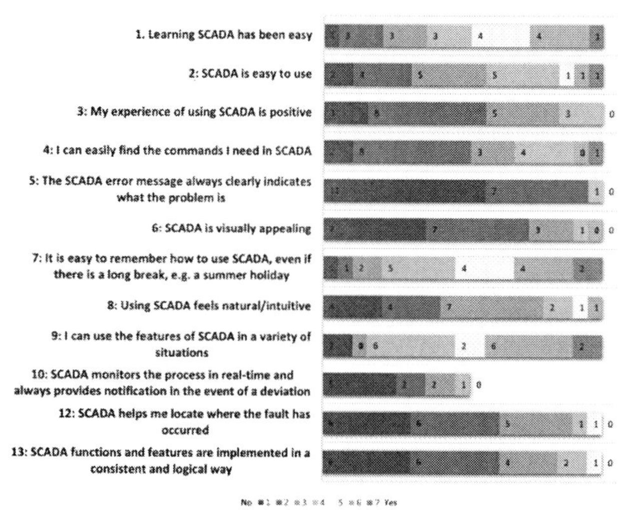

Figure 1. End-user survey questions and results

Figure 2. Survey results - Question 11 reversed scale

	Average	Question	Used attribute/metric (Table 1)	Observations
Usability achieved	5.21	11	Errors/User error protection (attribute 6)	
	4.68	9	Effectiveness (attribute 1)	
	4.58	7	Memorability (attribute 5)	
	4.16	1	Learnability (attribute 4)	
Identified areas for usability development	3.32	2	Operability (attribute 8)	1,3, 6, 7, 8, 10, 12
	2.94	4	Efficiency (attribute 2)	1, 4, 8, 11
	2.74	8	Intuitivity (attribute 13)	4
	2.42	3	Satisfaction (attribute 3)	2, 8, 10, 12
	2.26	13	Operability (attribute 8)	6, 7, 8, 12
	2.21	12	Supporting the user in decision making (attribute 12)	3, 9, 10, 12, 13
	2.11	6	User interface aesthetics (attribute 9)	10
	1.9	10	Up-to-date information (attribute 11)	3, 9, 10, 12, 13
	1.53	5	Supporting the user in decision making (attribute 12)	3, 9, 10, 12, 13

Figure 3. SCADA usability findings

Usability findings from operators
1. Slowness, stuttering, navigation is sometimes confusing and difficult
2. SCADA also has a lot of good things
3. Slowness of user interface in case of failures e.g. when moving from one page to another, you get used to using SCADA when using the system, it is easy to find the causes of failures
4. Requires learning by heart, no information is available when looking for a new thing and you have to rely on other operators
5. Needs further development
6. The system is confusing
7. Slow, illogical, production lines poorly outlined
8. System is confusing, difficult to find information, not enough information, several buttons not working or missing, slow to move from one page to
9. Operators are not consulted enough and requested changes are not implemented, fault locations are not clearly and accurately displayed
10. Poor visual appearance, poor navigation, poor alarm indication, some buttons missing, some buttons not working
11. Too much time spent moving from one page to another to access information and functions
12. Alarms poorly targeted, alarms can only be displayed on certain pages, alarm indication in main view should be better, not all information is accessible, SCADA implementations differ in views and functionalities
13. Operators have not been consulted enough and requested changes have not been implemented, and fault locations are not displayed clearly and accurately enough

Figure 4. The operators' observations and comments

Many respondents shared their own experiences, highlighting various usability issues. Specifically, 14 operators provided detailed opinions, user experiences, and usability observations in the survey's open comment field. Among the survey respondents, 93.8% had over a year of SCADA experience, lending credibility to their feedback. However, the small number of respondents per department prevented a comparative analysis of usability between production plants departments. Consequently, SCADA usability was analyzed at a holistic system level. This approach was validated by operator comments, which consistently highlighted similar experiences and usability observations across different departments.

SCADA usability was examined by dividing the survey statements into two categories based on average score (Figures

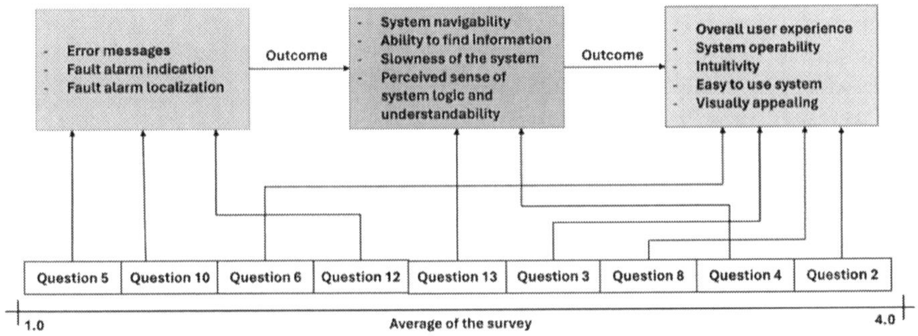

Figure 5. Root cause analysis of the cumulative effect resulting from process deviation

1 and 3): achieved usability characteristics (more than 4) and areas for improvement (less than 4). A Likert scale of 4 for neutral opinion was used as the cut-off value. For question 11 (Figure 2), the average was inverted because it was asked on an inverted Likert scale compared to other items. Figure 3 shows how the statements were distributed. The same table also shows which usability attribute or metric in Table I is referenced by the statement and which observation in Figure 4, provided by the operators, clearly refer to the statement.

The results in Figure 3 show that the average dispersion is weighted well below the neutral average, suggesting there is room for improvement in SCADA usability. The operator comments in the Figure 4 also reflect this observation. Although the averages are generally weighted below the neutral average, the responses to many of the survey and figure statements vary widely between the two extremes. This is an indication of the high degree of subjectivity in the user experience, especially in the areas around these statements.

Questions 1, 7, 9, and 11 exceeded the neutral average and are therefore considered functional and successful in describing their SCADA usability characteristics. Based on these statements, SCADA has been successfully implemented in a fault-tolerant manner so that human errors or their effects do not negatively affect the usability of the system (Q11). Operators also feel that they can use SCADA in a wide range of work situations (Q9). Furthermore, the system is easy to remember (Q7) and not challenging to learn. The operators' comments do not contradict these findings.

Questions 2-6, 8, 10, 12, and 13 are below the neutral average. Based on the usability characteristics described by these statements, the areas for improvement in SCADA usability are related to: system error messages and their understandability (Q5), fault alarm indication (Q10), perceived aesthetic satisfaction (Q6), fault alarm localization (Q12), perceived sense of system logic and understandability (Q13), negative user experiences (Q3), system intuitiveness (Q8), system navigability and ability to find information or commands (Q4), and difficulties of using the system (Q2). Issues that are clearly related to these statements also appear in the operators' comments, in Figure 4. A new finding of usability that emerges from the operator comments is the slowness of SCADA (operator observations 1, 3, 7, 8, 11). The survey results particularly indicate that the most important areas for improvement in SCADA usability are related to system performance under fault conditions (Q5, Q10, Q12).

Figures 1-3 provide a clear and easily interpretable overview of SCADA usability successes and areas for improvement. These are supported by the operator usability findings presented in Figure 4. However, the identified usability improvement areas must also be viewed in the context of the SCADA being a complete control system in operation and meeting its operational objectives.

VI. Discussion: The Importance of Understanding Context, Root-causes and Causality

The results were analyzed using personal first-hand SCADA experience and contextual insight into how SCADA systems operate. The small sample size (19) limits both the generalizability of our findings and their applicability in other operational environments accross different industries. The study shows that, across departments, SCADA usability issues primarily involve system performance under fault conditions, including error messages, fault alarms, navigability, information retrieval, and system slowness (questions in Figure 3: 5, 10, and 12, and operator observations in Figure 4: 1, 3, 7-13). Faults typically involve situations where the control system automatically responds to process conditions and stops production. In this case, the control system also requires the operator to make a decision or take an action before the process can resume. This can mean controlling the process via SCADA or physically working on the production line. Faults are caused by deviations in the automated production process, and in these cases the operator's task is to return the production process to its normal state and resume it as quickly as possible. The operator faces both problem-solving and time pressure, impacting perceived usability. It is crucial to note that usability results under fault conditions reflects only these specific situations, not the system's overall uptime performance.

The primary usability challenges that follow a production process deviation are error messaging, fault alarm indication, and fault alarm localization. These are related to the system's capability to provide initial assistance to the operator in making decisions related to the ongoing process deviation.

Consequently, problems with these primary usability challenges, if not mitigated, lead to secondary challenges, which in this case are system navigability, ability to find information, system slowness, and perceived sense of system logic and understandability. This illustrates the underlying logical and contextual relationship between different usability challenges (RQ).

Similarly, it can be interpreted that the causal relationship can also have a cumulative effect on other areas of perceived usability: overall user experience, system operability, intuitivity, system ease of use, and visual pleasantness (questions 2-4, 8, 13). Figure 5 illustrates the causal relationship and cumulative effect between usability challenges. Another finding related to this interpretation is that the averages in Figure 3 closely support the development of this cumulative effect. This shows that the primary usability challenges may be root causes that have a cumulative and cascading effect on other aspects of the user's experience with the system (RQ).

The goal of this study and industry survey was to establish robust measurement criteria based on academic research, which is critical to accurately assessing usability issues. By analyzing the results with industry insights, we can identify root causes and causal relationships, enabling targeted development activities to improve usability and address gaps. These results demonstrate that understanding the context of use is crucial for making accurate observations and drawing valid conclusions. Additionally, the cumulative effect and root-cause hypothesis offer a valuable perspective for usability analysis. This approach shifts the focus from merely interpreting usability metrics to understanding causality, making it highly practical and beneficial for the industry.

VII. Conclusion

This paper presents the results of a SCADA usability study conducted in the Finnish forestry company, highlighting the challenges of achieving optimal usability. The study revealed that despite the achievement of system goals and the successful implementation of the system, there can be a significant gap between the actual usability experienced by the end user and the way the system performs. An important finding is that understanding the contextual aspects of the user experience proved to be critical. While the attributes and measures used in the study generally capture various aspects of usability effectively, the findings highlight the importance of a thorough understanding of the operating environment and workflow to accurately identify and address usability issues.

References

[1] A. Mathur, A. Dabas, and N. Sharma, "Evolution from industry 1.0 to industry 5.0," in *2022 4th International Conference on Advances in Computing, Communication Control and Networking (ICAC3N)*, 2022, pp. 1390–1394.

[2] T. Pfeiffer, J. Hellmers, E. M. Schön, and J. Thomaschewski, "Empowering user interfaces for industrie 4.0," *Proceedings of the IEEE*, vol. 104, 2016.

[3] C. Sikora and R. Swan, "Perceived usability and system complexity," in *Proceedings. 3rd Asia Pacific Computer Human Interaction (Cat. No.98EX110)*, 1998, pp. 76–81.

[4] H. M. Hassan and G. H. Galal-Edeen, "From usability to user experience," in *2017 International Conference on Intelligent Informatics and Biomedical Sciences (ICIIBMS)*, 2017, pp. 216–222.

[5] D. Stone, C. Jarrett, M. Woodroffe, and S. Minocha, *User Interface Design and Evaluation*. Elsevier, 2014.

[6] ISO9241-11, "Iso/iec. 9241-14 ergonomic requirements for office work with visual display terminals," 1998.

[7] ISO25000:2014, "Iso/iec 25000:2014, systems and software engineering, systems and software quality requirements and evaluation (square)," 2014.

[8] D. Richards and I. Kelaiah, "Usability attributes in virtual learning environments," in *Proceedings of The 8th Australasian Conference on Interactive Entertainment: Playing the System*, ser. IE '12. New York, NY, USA: Association for Computing Machinery, 2012.

[9] V. Basili, L. Briand, D. Bianculli, S. Nejati, F. Pastore, and M. Sabetzadeh, "Software engineering research and industry: A symbiotic relationship to foster impact," *IEEE Software*, vol. 35, pp. 44–49, 9 2018.

[10] M. L. Bourguet, "Metrics-based evaluation of graphical user interface aesthetics: The segmentation problem," *ISS 2018 - Companion Proceedings of the 2018 ACM International Conference on Interactive Surfaces and Spaces*, pp. 31–38, 11 2018.

[11] L. Briand, D. Bianculli, S. Nejati, F. Pastore, and M. Sabetzadeh, "The case for context-driven software engineering research: Generalizability is overrated," *IEEE Software*, vol. 34, pp. 72–75, 2017.

[12] D. Marijan, "45 industry-academia research collaboration and knowledge co-creation: Patterns and anti-patterns," *ACM Trans. Softw. Eng. Methodol*, vol. 31, 2022.

[13] L. A. Hasan and K. T. Al-Sarayreh, "An integrated measurement model for evaluating usability attributes," pp. 1–6, 11 2015.

[14] J. Sulaiman, T. Zulkifli, K. S. K. Ibrahim, and N. K. M. Noor, "Implementing usability attributes in e-learning system using hybrid heuristics," *2009 International Conference on Information and Multimedia Technology, ICIMT 2009*, pp. 189–193, 2009.

[15] R. Muhtaseb, K. Lakiotaki, and N. Matsatsinis, "Applying a multicriteria satisfaction analysis approach based on user preferences to rank usability attributes in e-tourism websites," *Journal of Theoretical and Applied Electronic Commerce Research*, vol. 7, pp. 28–48, 12 2012.

[16] M. Zen, N. Burny, and J. Vanderdonckt, "A quality model-based approach for measuring user interface aesthetics with grace," *Proceedings of the ACM on Human-Computer Interaction*, vol. 7, 6 2023.

[17] J. Nielsen, *The Usability Engineering Lifecycle*. Elsevier, 1993.

[18] ISO25023:2016, "Iso/iec 25023:2016 systems and software engineering, systems and software quality requirements and evaluation (square), measurement of system and software product quality," 2016.

[19] S. Karnouskos, R. Sinha, P. Leitão, L. Ribeiro, and T. I. Strasser, "The applicability of iso/iec 25023 measures to the integration of agents and automation systems," 2018.

[20] ISO9126, "Iso/iec 9126 information technology-software product evaluation-quality characteristics and guidelines for their use," 1991.

[21] ISO25010:2023, "Iso/iec 25010:2023 systems and software engineering, systems and software quality requirements and evaluation (square), product quality model," 2016.

[22] ISO13407, "Iso/iec 13407, human-centred design processes for interactive systems," 1999.

[23] D. Marghescu, "Usability evaluation of information systems: A review of five international standards," *Information Systems Development*, pp. 131–142, 2009.

[24] J. Nielsen, "Usability metrics: Tracking interface improvements," *IEEE Software*, vol. 13, 1996.

[25] B. Schneiderman, *Designing the User Interface: Strategies for Effective Human-Computer Interaction (3rd ed.)*. Addison-Wesley., 1998.

[26] T. Suojanen, K. Koskinen, and T. Tuominen, "User-centered translation." Routledge, 2014.

[27] N. Bevan, J. Carter, J. Earthy, T. Geis, and S. Harker, "New iso standards for usability, usability reports and usability measures," vol. 9731, 2016.

[28] S. International, "What is scada?" 2024. [Online]. Available: https://scada-international.com/what-is-scada/

[29] E. Hozdić and I. Makovec, "Evolution of the human role in manufacturing systems: On the route from digitalization and cybernation to cognitization," *Applied System Innovation*, vol. 6, 2023.

[30] D. Mourtzis, J. Angelopoulos, and N. Panopoulos, "The future of the human–machine interface (hmi) in society 5.0," *Future Internet*, vol. 15, 2023.

A Study of Third-Party Tracking on Religious Websites

Henna Lohi, Sampsa Rauti, Panu Puhtila, Timi Heino, Sammani Rajapaksha
Department of Computing
University of Turku
Turku, Finland
e-mail: {hmlohi | sjprau | papuht | tdhein | syraja}@utu.fi

Abstract—**Websites give many advantages to a religious community, making religious practices more accessible and enabling communication and community-building. At the same time, the user's privacy needs to be protected. This is particularly true for the data about their religious beliefs. The General Data Protection Regulation has strict requirements on the processing of special categories of personal data, including data revealing an individual's religious beliefs. This paper presents a case study of websites of the largest religious community in Finland, the Evangelical Lutheran Church. We study the prevalence of third parties and potential data leaks on 31 websites of this church. Our findings show that several measures have been taken to protect the user's privacy by the church and website maintainers, such as introducing a common platform for the vast majority of the websites and replacing Google Analytics with Matomo. However, there were still some privacy concerns such as leaking data to Meta and vague privacy policies. This case study serves both as an example of how many correct measures have been taken to prevent privacy violations and how web developers and data protection officers can further improve data protection.**

Keywords-Third parties; web analytics; data leaks; religious websites; online privacy.

I. INTRODUCTION

The information and communication technology is used to deliver all kinds of services and information today. This also goes for religious communities that seek to improve communication, community building and the accessibility of religious practices [1]. Web-based services, in particular, help religious communities to easily share their beliefs and announce events online. This way, they can spread their message, teachings and practices to a wider audience [2][3]. Internet makes it possible for religious communities to extend their reach beyond physical boundaries [4]. The websites of religious communities benefit both current members and those interested in learning more about the religion or community.

Religious beliefs – at least in the largely secular academic world and in postmodernism – are usually regarded as private matters [5]. An argument can be made that this privacy should also extend to online spaces [6]. The General Data Protection Regulation (GDPR) also reinforces this idea, setting strict requirements on the processing of data concerning religious beliefs [7]. Processing such data is forbidden by default, and requires explicit consent or specific legal grounds to occur. Therefore, privacy is an important consideration and challenge when designing websites of religious communities. For example, modern websites often use third-party analytics services. The data collection carried out by these services can lead to the inadvertent disclosure of users' religious affiliations. Protecting sensitive personal data on religious websites requires special attention and care.

In this paper, we study what kinds of third-party services are used on 31 websites of the Evangelical Lutheran Church of Finland. We also examine whether sensitive data concerning users' religious beliefs is sent to third parties. By analyzing the outgoing network traffic generated when browsing the websites, we study whether these websites leak sensitive personal data to third parties. Additionally, we analyze whether the user is into accepting cookies and data collection with dark patterns and whether the user is adequately informed about potential data sharing occurring on these websites. Finally, we also gauge how well the church supports parishes in building websites that prioritize privacy by design.

The rest of the paper is structured as follows. Section II presents the prior work related to our study. Section III explains the study setting and methods. Section IV presents the results of our network traffic analysis, along with an assessment of dark patterns and privacy policies. Section V discusses the lessons learned from assessing the privacy of the studied religious websites and explores the implications of our findings. Finally, Section VI concludes the paper.

II. RELATED WORK

The body of literature on third-party tracking is large. The excessive and intrusive collection of sensitive data has generally been considered a problem [8]–[11] and only rarely a benefit to users [12]. In particular, third-party health data leaks have been widely covered in prior work [13]–[17]. Automatic tools have been build to detect third-party data leaks and assess website privacy [18][19]. Several studies also examine privacy policy documents and gauge how well users are informed of ongoing data collection [20]–[26]. While the topic of data collection and data leaks on websites has been explored widely in the research literature, it has not been studied very extensively in the context of religious websites.

Hoy et al. [27] studied the privacy violations happening in 102 USA-based websites of Christian parishes, and also presented a questionnaire to the parish leadership figures which prompted responses from 23% of them. The sample material of this study consisted of a mixture of different Christian nomination websites, including Lutherans, Methodists, Catholics and Baptists. Their results indicated that as many as 99% of the church websites collected personal identifying information. However, it must be noted that their research methodology was different from ours, as they focused much more on the information that the parishioners knowingly and willingly submitted to the websites, whereas we focus entirely on the use of website analytical tools to collect data.

Samarasinghe et al. [6] conducted a very large scale survey on religious websites from four major religions – Christianity, Buddhism, Islam and Hinduism – focusing on their cybersecurity and privacy aspects. This study was done by utilizing OpenWPM, which is an automated system for detection privacy violations developed by researcher Steven Englehardt [28], Uniform Resource Locator (URL) Classification which is web-based system used for categorization of websites, and VirusTotal, which is a web-based computer virus detection platform operated by Chronicle, a subsidiary of Google. With this technology, Samarasinghe et al. scanned 583 784 websites and ultimately chose 62 373 of them to be analyzed. Their results indicated, among other things, that 27.9% of the religious websites used tracking scripts, and 5.7% used tracking cookies to collect personal data on their users.

While our sample size is small compared to Samarasinghe et al., their methodology was also very different, and that the study of data leaks was only one aspect of their research. Their sample material also consisted of a much more heterogeneous material, comprising websites representing many different religious worldviews and organizations. In contrast, the current study focuses on a very specific religious online presence, the Lutheran parish and diocese websites operating in Finland, presenting multi-case study that delves deeper into a specific group of religious websites. Thus, while their study gives a wider perspective on the privacy behavior of the religious websites in general, ours offers detailed description of websites of one religious community, offering a more in-depth analysis of the privacy issues, third parties and data leaks.

III. Study Setting and Method

In this section, we explain how the study is conducted including the data sets selected, the methods used and the study scope.

A. Case and Website Selection

The Evangelical Lutheran Church of Finland was chosen to be studied because it has a strong connection with the state and is a large organization with hundreds of websites [29]. These include websites for parishes and dioceses around Finland and general websites of the church. The Evangelical Lutheran Church of Finland holds a special legal position as a national church (along with the Orthodox Church of Finland), and has the capability to tax its members. In 2023, over 3.5 million Finns belonged to the Evangelical Lutheran Church. This means that approximately 65.1% of Finns were members of the church. Because of the church's special role and large number of potential visitors, special attention should be paid to the privacy of the church's websites, and it was a logical choice for a multi-case study.

Altogether, the Evangelical Lutheran Church of Finland has 354 local parishes in 9 dioceses [30]. The set of websites to be studied was selected according to the following selection criteria:

- Two parish websites were chosen randomly from each diocese to have a diverse selection of websites from around the country.
- The websites of all 9 dioceses were also selected.
- All the parish websites that did not use the church's own web platform (Lukkari) were also included. As stand-alone websites, these were deemed more likely to include unique third parties and potential data leaks.
- The general top-level website of the church (evl.fi) was also included in the study.

Overall, 31 websites were chosen to be studied, 17 of which used the Lukkari platform. Because we are first and foremost studying data leaks as a phenomenon here, naming specific parishes or dioceses behind the websites serves no purpose. When necessary, the studied websites are referred to using pseudonyms WS1–WS31.

B. Recording the Network Traffic

Network traffic was recorded with Google Chrome Developer Tools, and saved in HAR (shorthand for HTTP Archive) log files. Upon entering the website, all caches were disabled to ensure that they would not disrupt the recording results. Also, all cookies were consented to. Initially, we accessed the landing page. Following this, we conducted a search using the search feature, if available, and examined other pages on the website, particularly those that might process sensitive personal data or reveal information about how the user practices religion.

All network traffic generated while navigating the website was recorded to determine whether there were any data leaks to third parties and to analyze the nature of this data. Only the HTTP requests directed to third parties (external domains outside the studied web service) were filtered for further inspection. We manually looked through each of the filtered requests to examine the payloads for leaks of sensitive personal data.

Because this study focuses on *personal data*, it is important to define it. According to GDPR and the Finnish Office of the Data Protection Ombudsman, "personal data" refers to "all data related to an identified or identifiable person" [31] [32]. This definition covers technical details like Internet Protocol (IP) addresses, device identifiers, location data, or any variable that helps to identify the user of the website. While all of these data items alone may not identify an individual, they can often be combined to make identification possible, and therefore fall under the definition of "personal data". Rather than the actual identifying data, however, in this study we focused on contextual data related to an identifiable person, most notably religious beliefs.

C. Analyzing the Recorded Network Traffic

When studying the recorded network traffic, we looked for the following two sensitive data leak types in the HTTP request payloads:

1) *Search terms.* Search terms are inputs that are usually freely decided by the user, so they can be sensitive. For example, on a parish's website, a user might search information about services held in that parish. This implies interest in ecclesiastic activities and may disclose religious beliefs.
2) *Page URLs.* The individual pages under the website can often reveal specific religious topics the user is interested in. Particularly, numerous different events, such as church services, may have their own separate pages within the website. This way, the religious beliefs and practices to which an individual adheres can be disclosed.

D. Dark Patterns and Privacy Policies

We also analyzed dark patterns, privacy policies and cookie consent banners found on the websites. Dark patterns, UI designs crafted to manipulate users into taking actions they might not otherwise choose, can cause users to inadvertently accept data collection. In this study, we specifically looked at three dark patterns, adapted from the "Report of the work undertaken by the Cookie Banner Taskforce" by European Data Protection Board [33]: 1) The first layer of the cookie consent banner does not offer a reject button, 2) pre-ticked boxes are present in the cookie banner or cookies settings, which can used to define cookie choices, and 3) The "Accept all" button is unfairly highlighted with color or contrast choices in order to attract users to click it.

Privacy policies and cookie consent banners available on the studied religious websites were examined to answer the following questions:

- Does the document clearly inform users that they can be uniquely identified as a result of data collection?
- Does the document clearly mention what personal data items are sent to third parties?
- Does the document name all the third parties receiving the user's personal data?
- Does the document mention that religious beliefs can be revealed as a result of sharing data?

IV. Results

This section exemplifies the results we collected using the above mentioned study methods and data.

A. The General Picture

When it comes to privacy of public sector websites in Finland, the Finnish Deputy Data Protection Ombudsman has stated that governmental agencies must "carefully consider what types of tracking technologies are necessary on their websites." Furthermore, developers of public sector websites should ensure that users are "able to use online services provided by authorities without data on their website visit ending up in commercial use, for example." [34] This statement from the Deputy Data Protection Ombudsman offers clear guidance on how to maintain balance between using tracking technologies and protecting user privacy.

The Evangelical Lutheran Church of Finland has improved the privacy of their websites as a result of the statement. The vast majority of all websites of the church use the common Lukkari platform [35], and Google Analytics formerly employed by this platform was replaced with Matomo in 2023 [36]. Although Google Analytics was widely used by church websites before this, the privacy has since been greatly improved, and the common platform serves to enforce robust privacy.

B. Network Traffic Analysis

Figure 1 represents the most serious leak types we detected: page URL and search term leaks in the 31 studied websites of the Evangelical Lutheran church. On the left, numbers represent the total data leaks (both page URL leaks and search term leaks) for each website. In the middle, data leaks are categorized into two categories, page URL leaks and search term leaks. On the right, the number of data leaks received by each third party is shown. As can be seen, page URL leaks occurred 16 times, and search term leaks 14 times. The recipients of the leaked data were Google, Meta and Siteimprove. It is not surprising that Google Analytics amounted to 50% of all page URL and search term leaks, as it has been proven to be the largest reason for tracking and data leaks happening in websites [37][6]. In the current study, however, Meta amounted only to 3 data leaks, while Siteimprove Analytics, a much smaller analytics provider, amounted to 12 leaks. The reason for this is that the websites did not use Meta's actual analytics service (Meta Pixel) but made use of social media plugins on the websites.

In total, only 12/31 (38.7%) of the studied websites exhibited leaks, which can be seen as a good result, especially considering we intentionally chose to include several websites more likely to contain data leaks in our data set, that is, websites not using the church's Lukkari platform. On average, the websites which did leak data had 2.5 data leaks per website, with the lowest number of leaks being 1 and the highest being 4.

It must be noted that there were some third parties that were not considered risky and thus not counted in data leaks. Firstly, the Matomo analytics service, which allows the website maintainer to retain the control over the data (although data may be stored on a remote server), was not counted. Rather than a harmful analytics service, it is a recommended service. Giosg, a popular chat service based in Finland was also not counted as a risky third party. Finally, Snoobi, a Finnish analytics service also widely used by public sector and state websites, was also excluded.

Matomo was found on 24/31 (77.4%) websites, which is a good result from privacy point of view. However, on many websites it was used along with other analytics services, which greatly undermines its privacy benefits. Still, compared to many other studies [37][38], the number of third parties (3) receiving sensitive data is exceptionally small, which speaks of decent privacy practices.

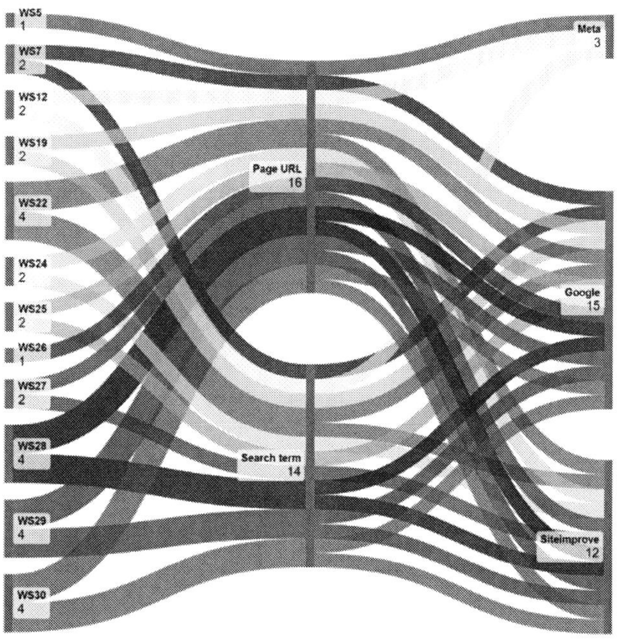

Figure 1. Data leaks detected on 12 different websites.

It is also worth noting that although not considered a highly serious data leak type here and not included in Figure 1, there were also website URL leaks in the studied pages. Although not as critical as the page URL and search term leaks discussed above, website URLs reveal that the user has visited a specific website (domain name). They do not give information on visiting specific subpages, but regular visits to the same website could still reveal the user's religious affiliation. The studied websites leaked the website URL to Meta 10 times, to Google 8 times and to Siteimprove 6 times. Finally, it is worth noting that there was also one third party, X/Twitter, which was present on more than half (16) of the studied websites as a social media plugin, but never received sensitive personal data such as visited pages.

Lastly, what makes the data leaks discussed here sensitive is the combination of identifying data (such as an IP address) and contextual data (such as a URL of a visited page). There are several reasons why an individual user can often be uniquely identified by third parties. First off, an IP address is a crucial piece of data for identifying users [39] and it is considered personal data in most cases [31]. Third parties can also identify users through cookies. For example, Google Analytics uses a cookie that lasts for 2 years and includes a unique client ID (cid) to distinguish users [40]. Google also uses cross-device tracking by leveraging data from logged-in Google accounts [41]. Similarly, Meta/Facebook uses accounts to keep track of users using different devices. Because of these technologies, users' actions and the pages they visit are not just linked to IP addresses, but in many cases, to actual names of individual persons.

C. *Privacy Policies, Cookie Consent Banners and Dark Patterns*

There were 4 websites that failed to name the third parties in their privacy policies or cookies consent banners, even though our network traffic analysis showed they had third parties present. Other 25 websites that had third parties present did mention these third parties either in their privacy policies or cookie consent banners, which is a positive result. However, we found that none of the websites collecting data informed the user adequately of the possibility of unique identification. Also, none of the privacy policies or cookie consent banners clearly mentioned that visited URLs or search terms are shared to third parties, even when this was often the case in reality. However, 8 websites vaguely mentioned collecting data on how the visitors use the website. Lastly, the possibility of religious beliefs leaking was never mentioned.

Privacy policies and cookie consent banners of all studied websites of the parishes were identical with each other, and those used by the dioceses except one were identical with each other. In other words, the parishes used one kind of template for these elements, and dioceses used another. However, the third parties the websites included varied.

In many sections of the privacy policies of the diocese websites, the possibility of data collection was explained in raw technical details that are difficult for the average website users to comprehend. This issue of privacy policies containing overly technical jargon has been recognized in prior research [42]. Also, many categorizations of the data collection methods were incorrect or highly ambiguous.

Privacy policies of the parishes, on the other hand, all linked to the same website containing the privacy policy, maintained by the Evangelical Lutheran Church of Finland [43]. This website listed all of the third parties present, and provided a short common language explanation for the cookies in use. However, it provided the details of the cookies used by linking to other websites, which were maintained by the proprietors of these analytics services. Most of these websites were in English, and all of them asked for permission to data collection, which can be seen as highly problematic in its own right. This forces the user to enter a third-party website and make a decision whether to allow the web analytics on that website to harvest their data, just to read how the cookies are used on the original parish website.

Out of 31 websites, 5 (16.1%) did not ask for consent for cookies and data collection at all, although they collected personal data. As a positive result, the rest of the studied cookie consent banners did offer a reject button on the first layer, and none of the banners had pre-ticked selection boxes. On 9 websites (29.0%), however, the cookie consent banners unfairly highlighted the accept button with prominent colors and contrast. It must be noted that the reject button was always labeled as "Allow only necessary", which could be considered slightly misleading. Also, the tickable consent boxes used in the cookie consent banners were colored light gray when the consent had been given, and black when not. This can be considered misleading since the usual convention is to use a lighter color for unchecked boxes and a darker color when it is checked. In essence, the common convention of using colors in website design was inverted in these banners.

V. Discussion

The results are further discussed in this section. The main discussion points are given as subsections.

A. Lessons Learned in Web Development

There are many lessons to be learned from the studied websites and their privacy practices. In what follows, we will explore both positive and negative aspects based on our findings.

1) Positive Aspects:

Following the privacy guidelines. The Evangelical Lutheran Church of Finland, unlike many other public sector bodies, has taken note of the Deputy Data Protection Ombudsman's statement on the use of third parties on the websites of public sector bodies and the careful consideration of necessary tracking technologies. This shows that guidelines and recommendations by data protection authorities have a significant effect on privacy in practice. While our findings and lessons learned are applicable to other religious communities in many respects, it is very likely that not all communities have followed privacy recommendations equally well. The same can be said of many other application areas, such as healthcare, where web-based systems often seem to lack much needed privacy measures.

Common platform and clear recommendations. The vast majority of the websites are using the same platform and the church strongly advocates employing a local analytics solution, Matomo, instead of Google Analytics. Matomo enables the church to control the collected data without sharing users' personal data with third parties [44][45]. Therefore, it is evident that although using a common platform can sometimes have negative effects to privacy by introducing or making it easy to include third-party analytics [46], it can also prevent data leaks when done correctly.

Getting rid of Google Analytics. Taking advantage of the commonly used platform, the church has systematically phased out Google Analytics, which has been seen to be a problematic (and even illegal) web analytics solution based on the Deputy Data Protection Ombudsman's statement.

Migrating away from third-party analytics. The case of Evangelical Lutheran Church of Finland also demonstrates that data collected with Google Analytics can be migrated to Matomo, even though it is not a quick and entirely straightforward process, when there is lots of gathered data.

Using a small set of third-party services. The church websites only made use of a very small number of third-party services, and data only leaked to 3 third parties. This makes it possible to scrutinize the used services more closely and improves user privacy.

2) Issues to be Addressed:

Not consistently using the common platform and failing to follow recommendations. Some of the parish websites did not use the provided Lukkari platform, even though it has been available for about 10 years. Moreover, some of the websites not built with the platform still used Google Analytics, although its use is discouraged both by the church and data protection authorities.

Ignoring risky third parties Another problem is ignoring privacy issues caused by certain third parties even when the common platform is used. Most notably, URL addresses of visited pages leaked to Meta on two websites using the Lukkari platform. It can be argued that Meta is as problematic a data collector as Google is. Earlier studies have suggested that Meta has commercially exploited potentially sensitive personal data for advertising purposes [47]. From this viewpoint, we argue it is quite obvious that the previously mentioned Deputy Data Protection Ombudsman's statement should also be applied to Meta and Meta's services should not be used on pages processing sensitive data if they leak the page URL.

Vague privacy policies. All the studied websites used privacy policy documents that were generic and unclear at many points. For example, as the third parties used on the websites vary, privacy policies should also reflect this by clearly mentioning the used third-party services. Users should be able to find out what kind of personal data is being sent out and to which third parties it is being shared. The privacy policies should mention that the visited pages and their topics can leak to third parties, some of which may be processing data outside of Europe.

Inadequate consent. Not all websites asked for consent for cookies and data collection. This violates the GDPR when the website uses cookies [48]. Leaking data concerning religious beliefs is especially serious when no consent is asked. Even when a general consent for data collection was requested, data concerning religious beliefs was never specifically mentioned and it is unlikely the user expects this kind of information to be shared with third parties.

B. Implications for Users

When a website leaks a user's religious affiliation to a third party, the user's privacy is violated. The user's personal beliefs are shared and revealed, often without their explicit permission. As a result of this, users may feel they have lost control over their personal information. The leaked data concerning religion can be used in targeted advertising or attempts to persuade people [49]. It is possible that some actors might try to change a person's religious or political views based on the gathered data. Obviously, these kinds of actions raise ethical concerns and go against an individual's right to make their own choices.

In certain societies, people might face prejudice or unfair treatment due to their faith when others find out about it [50]–[52]. This unfair treatment can manifest in different ways, like being left out or not getting hired for jobs. In extreme cases, sensitive religious data leaked could even put people at risk if malicious actors get their hands on it. While this may be unlikely, the simple fact that these possible dangers exist is enough reason to prevent careless sharing of sensitive personal data.

Website visitors may also stop trusting their religious group if their sensitive personal data is leaked to third parties. This can hurt relationships between community members and make them doubt their leaders. Moreover, leaking an individual's religious beliefs can cause them a lot of pain and anxiety. Religious communities that let such data fall into wrong hands could also face legal problems.

VI. Conclusion

To conclude, findings of this study are promising in regards to user privacy. The number of third parties and privacy issues detected was relatively small when compared to other studies and categories of websites [6][37]. This is mainly the result of the Evangelical Lutheran Church of Finland having an organization-wide policy of using the same platform for the majority of their websites, which significantly reduces the number of third-party services in use. While using a common platform does not always result in a positive outcome, in this particular case it has resulted in uniform adoption of stringent privacy practices, which can in many ways be considered a recommendable outcome.

Still, several websites were found to leak personal data potentially revealing the user's religious beliefs to third parties such as Google and Meta. This was because all websites did not use the common Lukkari platform provided by the church but also because this platform still allowed third parties like Meta and Siteimprove to be present. This is why an external privacy audit would still be a good idea for the websites processing sensitive data like religious beliefs. Avoiding dark patterns and aiming for the clarity and comprehensiveness of privacy policies are also areas where corners can not be cut. As future work, we plan to extend this examination to other religious communities.

Acknowledgments

This research has been funded by Academy of Finland project 327397, IDA – Intimacy in Data-Driven Culture.

References

[1] O. Golan and N. Stadler, "Building the sacred community online: The dual use of the internet by chabad," *Media, culture & society*, vol. 38, no. 1, pp. 71–88, 2016.

[2] P. H. Cheong, J. P. Poon, S. Huang, and I. Casas, "The internet highway and religious communities: Mapping and contesting spaces in religion-online," *The Information Society*, vol. 25, no. 5, pp. 291–302, 2009.

[3] T. Hutchings, "Contemporary religious community and the online church," *Information, Communication & Society*, vol. 14, no. 8, pp. 1118–1135, 2011.

[4] A. Vitullo, "Multisite churches. creating community from the offline to the online," *Online-Heidelberg Journal of Religions on the Internet*, 2019.

[5] D. Shatz, "On Undermining the Beliefs of Others: Religion and the Ethics of Persuasion," *Faith: Jewish Perspectives*, pp. 137–187, 2013.

[6] N. Samarasinghe, P. Kapoor, M. Mannan, and A. Youssef, "No salvation from trackers: Privacy analysis of religious websites and mobile apps," in *International Workshop on Data Privacy Management*, Springer, 2022, pp. 151–166.

[7] GDPR-info.eu, *Processing of special categories of personal data*, https://gdpr-info.eu/art-9-gdpr/, Accessed: 2024-08-22, 2024.

[8] T. Wambach and K. Bräunlich, "The evolution of third-party web tracking," in *Information Systems Security and Privacy: Second International Conference, ICISSP 2016, Rome, Italy, February 19-21, 2016, Revised Selected Papers 2*, Springer, 2017, pp. 130–147.

[9] P. M. Schwartz, "Privacy, ethics, and analytics," *IEEE security & privacy*, vol. 9, no. 3, pp. 66–69, 2011.

[10] A. R. Zheutlin, J. D. Niforatos, and J. B. Sussman, "Data-tracking on government, non-profit, and commercial health-related websites," *Journal of general internal medicine*, pp. 1–3, 2021.

[11] A. Chandler and M. Wallace, "Using Piwik instead of Google analytics at the Cornell university library," *The Serials Librarian*, vol. 71, no. 3-4, pp. 173–179, 2016.

[12] I. Kes, D. Heinrich, and D. M. Woisetschlager, "Behavioral targeting in health care marketing: Uncovering the sunny side of tracking consumers online," in *Let's Get Engaged! Crossing the Threshold of Marketing's Engagement Era: Proceedings of the 2014 Academy of Marketing Science (AMS) Annual Conference*, Springer, 2016, pp. 297–297.

[13] M. D. Huesch, "Privacy threats when seeking online health information," *JAMA Internal Medicine*, vol. 173, no. 19, pp. 1838–1840, 2013.

[14] M. Huo, M. Bland, and K. Levchenko, "All eyes on me: Inside third party trackers' exfiltration of phi from health-care providers' online systems," in *Proceedings of the 21st Workshop on Privacy in the Electronic Society*, ACM, 2022, pp. 197–211.

[15] A. Surani *et al.*, "Security and privacy of digital mental health: An analysis of web services and mobile apps," in *Conference on Data and Applications Security and Privacy*, 2023.

[16] X. Yu, N. Samarasinghe, M. Mannan, and A. Youssef, "Got sick and tracked: Privacy analysis of hospital websites," in *2022 IEEE European Symposium on Security and Privacy Workshops (EuroS&PW)*, IEEE, 2022, pp. 278–286.

[17] A. R. Zheutlin, J. D. Niforatos, and J. B. Sussman, "Data-tracking on government, non-profit, and commercial health-related websites," *Journal of general internal medicine*, vol. 37, no. 5, pp. 1315–1317, 2022.

[18] V. Wesselkamp *et al.*, "In-depth technical and legal analysis of tracking on health related websites with ernie extension," in *Proceedings of the 20th Workshop on Workshop on Privacy in the Electronic Society*, ACM, 2021, pp. 151–166.

[19] R. Carlsson, P. Puhtila, and S. Rauti, *Towards an automatic tool for detecting third-party data leaks on websites*, Accepted to the 10th Workshop on Software Quality Analysis, Monitoring (SQAMIA2023), 2023.

[20] G. P. Dias, H. Gomes, and A. Zúquete, "Privacy policies and practices in portuguese local e-government," *Electronic Government, an International Journal*, vol. 12, no. 4, pp. 301–318, 2016.

[21] K. Schnell and R. Kaushik, "Hunting for the privacy policy – hospital website design," SSRN Elsevier, 2022.

[22] S. D. Brown and Y. Levy, "Towards a development of an index to measure pharmaceutical companies' online privacy practices," *Online Journal of Applied Knowledge Management (OJAKM)*, vol. 1, no. 1, pp. 93–108, 2013.

[23] T. Kautto and P. Henttonen, "Availability and findability of FOI and privacy statements on Finnish municipalities' websites," *Tidskriftet Arkiv*, vol. 8, no. 1, 2017.

[24] J. Burkell and A. Fortier, "Privacy policy disclosures of behavioural tracking on consumer health websites," in *Proceedings of the American Society for Information Science and Technology*, vol. 50, Wiley Online Library, 2013, pp. 1–9.

[25] A. Beldad, M. de Jong, and M. Steehouder, "Reading the least read? indicators of users' intention to consult privacy statements on municipal websites," *Government Information Quarterly*, vol. 27, no. 3, pp. 238–244, 2010, ISSN: 0740-624X.

[26] K. Schuele, "Privacy policy statements on municipal websites," *The Journal of Government Financial Management*, vol. 54, no. 2, pp. 20–29, 2005.

[27] M. G. Hoy and J. Phelps, "Consumer privacy and security protection on church web sites: Reasons for concern," *Journal of Public Policy & Marketing*, vol. 22, no. 1, pp. 58–70, 2003.

[28] S. Englehardt, "Automated discovery of privacy violations on the web," Ph.D. dissertation, Princeton, NJ: Princeton University, 2018.

[29] Evangelical Lutheran Church of Finland, *Published websites*, https://lukkariohje.evlut.fi/tietoa-lukkarista/julkaistut, Accessed: 2024-08-22, 2024.

[30] Evangelical Lutheran Church of Finland, *Parishes*, https://evl.fi/en/the-church/organisation/parishes/, Accessed: 2024-08-22, 2024.

[31] Office of the Data Protection Ombudsman, *What is personal data?* https://tietosuoja.fi/en/what-is-personal-data, Accessed: 2024-08-22, 2024.

[32] GDPR.eu, *What is considered personal data under the EU GDPR?* https://gdpr.eu/eu-gdpr-personal-data/, Accessed: 2024-08-22, 2024.

[33] European Data Protection Board, *Report on Work Undertaken by the Cookie Banner Taskforce*, https://edpb.europa.eu/our-work-tools/our-documents/other/report-work-undertaken-cookie-banner-taskforce_en, Accessed: 2024-08-22, 2024.

[34] Office of the Data Protection Ombudsman, *Deputy Data Protection Ombudsman Issues Reprimand for Conveying Library Search Information to US-Based Google*, https://tietosuoja.fi/en/-/deputy-data-protection-ombudsman-issues-reprimand-for-conveying-library-search-information-to-us-based-google, Accessed: 2024-08-22, 2024.

[35] Evangelical Lutheran Church of Finland, *Lukkari-ohje*, https://lukkariohje.evlut.fi/, Accessed: 2024-08-22, 2024.

[36] Evangelical Lutheran Church of Finland, *Kävijäanalytiikka*, https://lukkariohje.evlut.fi/yleiset-ohjeet/kavijaanalytiikka, Accessed: 2024-08-22, 2024.

[37] T. Heino, S. Rauti, R. Carlsson, and V. Leppänen, "Study of third-party analytics services on university websites," in *International Conference on Hybrid Intelligent Systems*, Springer, 2022, pp. 1284–1292.

[38] A. Vänskä *et al.*, "Fair data is the new black: Online shopping, data leaks, and broadening the understanding of sustainable fashion," *Fashion Theory*, pp. 1–29, 2024.

[39] V. Mishra *et al.*, "Don't count me out: On the relevance of ip address in the tracking ecosystem," in *Proceedings of The Web Conference 2020*, 2020, pp. 808–815.

[40] Google, *How google uses cookies*, https://policies.google.com/technologies/cookies?hl=en-US, Accessed: 2024-08-22, 2024.

[41] Google, *[GA4] Activate Google signals for Google Analytics 4 properties*, https://support.google.com/analytics/answer/9445345?hl=en, Accessed: 2024-08-22, 2024.

[42] C. D. Asay, "Consumer information privacy and the problems (s) of third-party disclosures," *Nw. J. Tech. & Intell. Prop.*, vol. 11, p. 321, 2012.

[43] Evangelical Lutheran Church of Finland, *Evästeiden käyttö verkkosivuilla*, https://evl.fi/tietosuoja/evasteet/, Accessed: 2024-08-22, 2024.

[44] J. Gamalielsson *et al.*, "Towards open government through open source software for web analytics: The case of matomo," *JeDEM-eJournal of eDemocracy and Open Government*, vol. 13, no. 2, pp. 133–153, 2021.

[45] D. Quintel and R. Wilson, "Analytics and privacy," *Information Technology and Libraries*, vol. 39, no. 3, 2020.

[46] S. Rauti *et al.*, "Analyzing third-party data leaks on online pharmacy websites," *Health and Technology*, pp. 1–18, 2024.

[47] J. G. Cabañas, Á. Cuevas, and R. Cuevas, "Unveiling and quantifying facebook exploitation of sensitive personal data for advertising purposes," in *27th USENIX security symposium (USENIX security 18)*, 2018, pp. 479–495.

[48] T. Wei, C. Cao, and Y. Shi, "Personal information protection behaviors of consumers in different country context and user interface designs," in *International Conference on Human-Computer Interaction*, Springer, 2022, pp. 82–98.

[49] Á. Cuevas, J. G. Cabañas, A. Arrate, and R. Cuevas, "Does facebook use sensitive data for advertising purposes? worldwide analysis and dgpr impact," *arXiv preprint arXiv:1907.10672*, 2019.

[50] J. L. Roberts, "Protecting privacy to prevent discrimination," *Wm. & Mary L. Rev.*, vol. 56, pp. 2097–2175, 2014.

[51] F. A. Whitlock and J. Hynes, "Religious stigmatization: An historical and psychophysiological enquiry," *Psychological Medicine*, vol. 8, no. 2, pp. 185–202, 1978.

[52] V.-I. Savic, "GDPR and Religious Freedoms (With Insight Into Ronald Dworkin and Competing Rights)," *CEJCL*, vol. 3, p. 115, 2022.

Building Model-Based Code Generators for Lower Development Costs and Higher Reuse

Hans-Werner Sehring
Department of Computer Science
NORDAKADEMIE gAG Hochschule der Wirtschaft
Elmshorn, Germany
e-mail: sehring@nordakademie.de

Abstract—**Model-driven software development is gaining attention due to the various benefits it promises. Typical approaches start with the modeling of application domains and continue with the specification of software to be developed. Model transformations are applied to develop and refine artifacts. In a final step, executable code is generated from models. Practice shows that model-based code generators have to bridge a rather large gap between the most refined software models and executable code implementing these models. This makes the development of code generators themselves an expensive task. In this article, we discuss ways to break down the development of code generators into smaller steps. Our discussion is guided on the one hand by principles of compiler construction and on the other hand by an application of model-driven development itself. Using a sample modeling language, we demonstrate how code generation can be organized to reduce development costs and increase reuse.**

Keywords—software development; software engineering; symbolic execution; top-down programming.

I. INTRODUCTION

Software construction requires methods and processes that guide development from an initial problem statement through all stages of the software lifecycle, culminating in the implementation, testing, roll-out, operations, and maintenance of the software.

Model-Driven Software Engineering (*MDSE*) strives to support such development processes by making explicit

- the artifacts created in each stage and possibly intermediate results
- the decisions that lead to the development of each artifact.

Ideally, MDSE supports the entire software lifecycle from requirements engineering and domain concepts through software architecture, design, and programming to software operations.

Figure 1 outlines some typical artifacts of software engineering processes. While many of them can be handled in MDSE processes, executable code must be generated for a particular target platform, such as a *Programming Language* (*PL*), software libraries, a runtime environment, and a target infrastructure. Later stages that depend on code, for example, operations tasks, also must be considered in code generation. This prepares code for activities like maintenance, monitoring, etc.

The support provided by MDSE approaches has advantages in many application areas. Models of sufficient formality can be checked for completeness or correctness to a certain extent. Traceability between artifacts allows to understand design decisions and model transformation steps during software maintenance. A final step of automated generation of executable code can save development costs during the implementation phase. Fully automated generation allows incremental development through model changes if the software is generated in an evolution-friendly manner.

Therefore, code generation from software models allows to take advantage of the potential benefits of modeling in MDSE. However, experience shows that generator development tends to be complex and costly. We see different reasons for this.

- The abstraction that models provide over programming language expressions require code generators to deal with a higher level of abstraction than compilers for PLs.
- Implementation details that are not reasonably part of software models must be added in code during generation.
- Various non-functional requirements of professional software development must be satisfied by generated code in addition to the requirements explicitly reflected by the software models. A code generator must add code for these as cross-cutting concerns.

Furthermore, these aspects of code generation typically require the development of project-specific generators.

Code generators are similar to compilers for high-level PLs. From this point of view, a model-driven process can be divided into a *frontend* and a *backend* part. In this logical division, the frontend deals with the more abstract models of the application domain and software design in *model-to-model transformations* (*M2MTs*). These early phases are covered by MDSE approaches. The backend activities of code generation, optimization, and target platform considerations are often hidden in implementations of comprehensive *model-to-text transformations* (*M2TTs*).

In this paper, we propose a structure for decomposing code generator development for easier development and a higher level of reuse.

The remainder of this paper is organized as follows: In Section II, we review model-driven software engineering with a focus on the final step of code generation. A corresponding approach to code generation is outlined in Section III. In Section IV, we illustrate the model-driven code generation approach with some sketches of code generation models. The paper is concluded in Section V.

II. MODEL-DRIVEN SOFTWARE DEVELOPMENT

In this section, we revisit MDSE in general and code generation in particular in order to lay the foundation for the discussion of model-based code generation in the following sections.

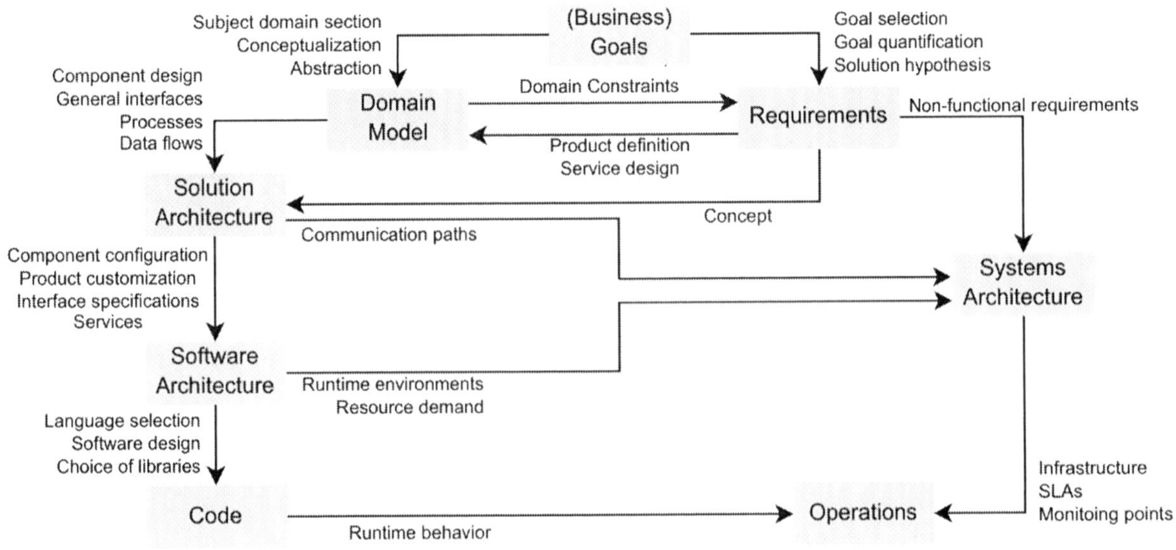

Figure 1. Typical software engineering artifacts.

A. *Software Modeling*

Models of the early steps in the software lifecycle are formulated from the perspective of the application domain. We do not consider domain models in this paper.

B. *Cases of Code Generation*

We see two application scenarios for software construction with MDSE:

1) approaches for systems of a given application class that share fixed functionality at some level of abstraction
2) approaches for application-specific functionality

A typical case of an application class with fixed functionality is the case of information systems, that typically provide only *Create, Read, Update, Delete* (*CRUD*) operations. Models of information systems, therefore, mainly represent domain entities and their relationships. Software generation is based on fixed patterns for code that provides CRUD functionality for the various entities.

Approaches that can be found in the class of generators that produce code with fixed functionality work with meta-programming [1], template-based approaches (see below), and combinations of these two [2]. Since generators for a specific target implementation can be built in a generic way, MDSE can be employed comparatively easy in this scenario.

In the general case of software containing custom business logic, software must be generated according to specified functionality. To automatically derive working software from specifications, MDSE approaches for application-specific business functionality must include formal models for precise definitions.

Means for deriving software from formal models are often built into editing tools for the respective formalisms. With respect to running software, formal models are typically used in one of two ways: Either code is generated from such models, or hand-written code is embedded in formal models at specific extension points.

For production-grade software systems, code generation is the only option in order to satisfy nonfunctional requirements.

A practical software system consists of different components, each of which is typically created by one generator each. Therefore, multiple code generators need to work in concert. To this end, different generator runs have to be orchestrated [2], and information exchange (for example, for identifiers used in different components) has to be managed [1].

C. *Code Generation Techniques*

Code is generated in a final step of an MDSE process, often based on M2TTs [3].

Special attention is paid to code generation, as this step can be well formalized in an MDSE process. There are several techniques for code generation, mainly generic code generators, meta-programming, and template-based techniques. Generative AI could be an alternative.

This way, there is reuse of software generators that translate formal specifications into code in a generic way. Typically, there is little or no way to direct the code generation for the case at hand [4]. Therefore, the generated code must be wrapped in order to be integrated into a production-grade software system, for example, to add error handling and additional code for monitoring.

a) Generic Code Generators: Custom functionality generally needs to be formulated in a Turing-complete formalism. Although the ability to verify such descriptions is limited, their expressiveness is required. Formal specifications of software functionality can be translated into working software by a code generator, that works like a compiler for a PL.

Code generators of modeling tools provide a well-tested and generally applicable translation facility. Specifications according to a given formalism are translated into a supported target environment. Examples include parser generators that generate code from grammars, software generators that take finite state machines as input [5], and those that use Petri Nets to execute code on firing transitions [6].

Generic code generators require significant development effort. But they can be developed centrally in a generic way. Therefore, there is a high degree of code reuse in the form of generators. However, the models used as input are application-specific, and they must be more elaborate than the input for other forms of generators.

b) Meta-Programming: Programs that generate programs are an obvious means of generating software. Meta-programming is possible with PLs, that allow the definition of data structures that represent code and from which code can be emitted. Since many widely used languages do not include meta-programming facilities, this capability is added through software libraries or at the level of development environments.

Meta-programming provides maximum freedom in generating custom code. Consequently, results can be tailored to the application at hand, including specific business logic.

However, the development of such generators tends to be costly, depending on the degree of individuality of code. This is due to the fact that meta-programs are harder to maintain and to debug due to their abstract nature. In addition, code reuse is very low for custom code.

c) Templates: Code with recurring structures can be formulated as templates with parameters for the variations of this uniform code. Code is generated by applying the templates with different parameter values.

A prominent example of a template-based approach is used for the *Model-Driven Architecture (MDA)*. The *MOF Model to Text Transformation Language* [7] provides a means to define code templates based on (UML) models.

Templates are easy to write, depending on the degree of generics. They allow adaptation to the project at hand by making changes to templates. The degree of reuse of templates within a project can be high, depending of the structural similarities between parts of the code. Cross-project reuse can be expected to be quite low.

d) Generative AI: The currently emerging generative AI approaches based on large language models provide another way to generate code from descriptions. Based on a library of examples, they allow the interactive generation of code from less formal descriptions, especially natural language expressions.

Generative AI can deal with complex requirements and rules. It has the advantage of being able to generate code in multiple PLs from (almost) the same descriptions.

There are indications that generative AI may be particularly well suited to producing code on a small scale, for example, individual modules [8]. Final quality assurance and assembly currently remains a manual task.

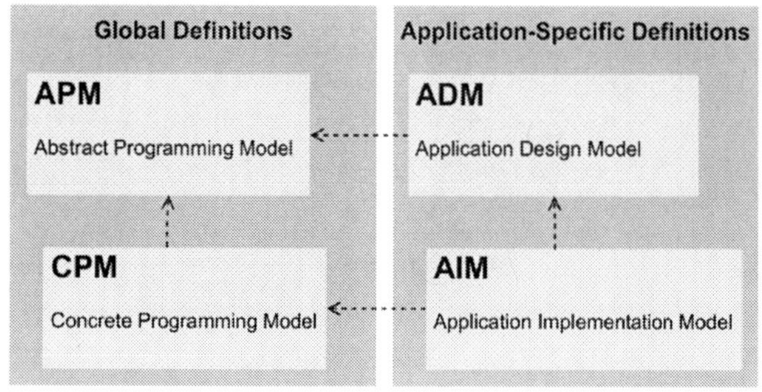

Figure 2. Code models and their relationships.

Instead of generating the actual software solution, generative AI can also be used to create code generators [3].

III. Model-Based Code Generation

In this paper, we discuss a way to construct code through a series of model refinement steps and final code generation. Thus, it follows the typical theme of M2MTs followed by an M2TT. However, our goal is to make the code generation step nearly trivial and fully automatic. To achieve this, we propose certain code models that bridge the gap between domain or solution models and executable code.

Our goal is to reduce the complexity of generators through abstraction and to reduce costs through reuse of *abstract code*.

Figure 2 gives an overview of the kinds of code models. Those in *Global Definitions* are provided centrally as a kind of modeling framework. Those in *Application-Specific Definitions* are models that are provided for each software project.

The four model boxes in the figure represent classes of models. There will be several concrete models for each of them.

We describe the models in the following subsections. Examples are given in the following main section.

The outline of the approach is as follows:

- Abstraction leads to a hierarchy of models.
- An *Abstract Program Model (APM)* provides a generic model of code.
- An *Application Design Model (ADM)* defines the functionality of a software system in terms of an APM.
- A *Concrete Program Model (CPM)* serves as a technology model; it maps an APM to a concrete implementation technology, such as a PL
- An *Application Implementation Model (AIM)* is used for code generation; it provides a project-specific association of the desired functionality and a technology model

With these models, some degree of reuse is achieved on the level of

1) programming models / building blocks of abstract programs
2) idioms and design patterns for refactoring and optimizing abstract programs
3) code generation from abstract representations of the constructs of a particular PL into code

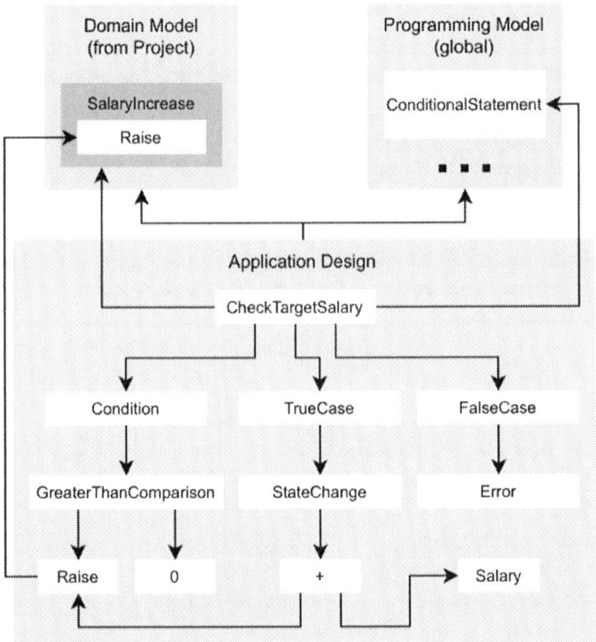

Figure 3. Typical software engineering artifacts.

A. *Models of Programming*

APMs serve as meta-models for abstract programs. Programming paradigms constitute a possible starting point for describing programming in general. Models of paradigms help to capture the essence of a class of PLs.

Properties of hybrid languages can be captured by combining models of programming paradigms. To this end, the modeling language used should allow models to be combined, and paradigm models must be set up to allow combinations.

There are differences between existing PLs that cannot be captured within one central model of programming. For example, object-oriented PLs have different ways of handling multiple inheritance. Therefore, there may be coexisting programming models, even for the same programming paradigm.

B. *Assigning Functionality to Domain Models*

In contrast to pure programming, program models in an MDSE process refer to more abstract models, especially those formulated from an application domain perspective. Program models result from M2MTs, or they refer to source models. Resulting model relationships are a basis for traceability [9].

Figure 3 illustrates a model relationship. A hypothetical domain model contains a *SalaryIncrease* concept with a *Raise* sub-concept . This specification is to be implemented using an imperative programming language, so there is, for example, a *ConditionalStatement*. The resulting model of the code for the software is represented as an ASM with a procedure *CheckTargetSalary*.

Application design models are essentially attributed syntax trees. In a kind of "reverse programming", we manually construct syntax trees and generate code from them. This is not the right level for manual development of software generators. But program models can be derived from domain models similar to template-based software generation. The example in Figure 3 can be viewed this way. The advantage of abstract models and model relations over code templates is the independence from concrete programming languages. This allows us to make an early connection between a domain and a code model while still having the option of choosing the implementation details, including the programming language or other implementation technologies to be used.

C. *Stepwise Refinement of Programming Models*

Concrete models define which language constructs are available in a particular PL that is selected for implementation. For code generation, the abstract application code (ASM) is combined with a CPM containing models of typical programming language constructs / idioms etc. in generalized form. M2MTs are applied to the combined model to transform it into an AIM that is suitable for code generation.

Model transformation consists of refining abstract program models with respect to a concrete PL or other implementation technology. There are several reasons why concrete models differ from abstract programming models. For example, there are different ways to implement abstract code in concrete PLs, similar PLs may have different best practices, they may have different constraints, and they may require different optimizations.

The transformation from an abstract to a concrete program need not be done in one step. For example, there is typically a hierarchy of abstractions, from abstract programs at the programming paradigm level, to classes of PLs and PL families, to concrete PLs, PL implementations or dialects, or even project-specific style guides.

D. *Generating Code from Abstract Programs*

An AIM is a model of a program that is suitable for code generation. This means, that all parts of a model are assigned a concrete PL expression and thus a syntactic form.

With this model property, code can be generated by assembling pieces of code that each represent model entities.

IV. Examples of Model Definitions for Code

We outline some models in order to illustrate the approach presented in the previous section. We use the *Minimalistic Meta Modeling Language* (*M³L*) as our modeling notation. This language is briefly introduced in order to discuss some model sketches.

A. *M³L Overview*

The M³L is a (meta) modeling language that has been reported about. Definitions are of the general form

```
A is a B { C is a D } |= E { F } |- G H .
```

Such a statement matches or creates a *concept* A. All parts of such a statement except the concept name are optional.

The concept *A* is a *refinement* of the concept *B*. Using the "is the" clause instead defines a concept as the only specialization of its base concept.

```
Type
Boolean is a Type
True is a Boolean False is a Boolean
Integer is a Type
Variable { Name Type }
Procedure { FormalParameter Statement }
Statement
ConditionalStatement is a Statement {
  Condition     is a Boolean
  ThenStatement is a Statement
  ElseStatement is a Statement }
Loop is a Statement { Body is a Statement}
HeadControlledLoop is a Loop {
  Condition is a Boolean }
VariableDeclaration is a Statement {
  Variable InitialValue is an Expression }
ProcedureCall is a Statement {
  Procedure ActualParameter}
Expression is a Statement ...
```

Figure 4. Sample base model of procedural programming.

```
IfTrueStmt is a ConditionalStatement {
  True is the Condition
} |= ThenStatement
IfFalseStmt is a ConditionalStatement {
  False is the Condition
} |= ElseStatement
```

Figure 5. Semantics of conditional statements.

The concept C is defined in the *context* of A; C is part of the *content* of A. Each context defines a scope, and scopes are hierarchical. Concepts like A are defined in an unnamed top-level context.

There can be multiple statements about a concept with a given name in a scope. All visible statements about a concept are cumulated. This allows concepts to be defined differently in different contexts.

Semantic rules can be defined on concepts, denoted by "|=". A semantic rule references another concept, that is returned when a concept with a semantic rule is referenced.

Context, specializations, and semantic rules are employed for *concept evaluation*. A concept evaluates to the result of its syntactic rule, if defined, or to its *narrowing*. A concept B is a narrowing of a concept A if

- A evaluates to B through specializations or semantic rules, and
- the whole content of A narrows down to content of B.

Concepts can be marshalled/unmarshalled as text by *syntactic rules*, denoted by "|-". A syntactic rule names a sequence of concepts whose representations are concatenated. A concept without a syntactic rule is represented by its name. Syntactic rules are used to represent a concept as a string as well as to create a concept from a string.

```
Expression
Value is an Expression
ConditionalExpression is an Expression {
  Condition  is an Expression
  TrueValue  is an Expression
  FalseValue is an Expression }
Function is a Value {
  FormalParameter FunTerm }
FunCall is an Expression {
  Function ActualParameterList }
PartialFunCall is a FunCall, a Value
```

Figure 6. Sample base model of functional programming.

```
MetaClass is an Object { Method }
Method { Parameter is an Object }
Classifier is a MetaClass
Interface is a Classifier
AbstractClass is a Classifier
ConcreteClass is a Classifier
ObjectClass is a ConcreteClass
Object is an ObjectClass
```

Figure 7. Sample base model of object-oriented programming.

B. Example Programming Models

Sticking with the example of starting the modeling of programming with programming paradigms, there may be models that describe typical constructs of PLs of a particular paradigm. We give short outlines of PL base models for the most important programming paradigms. Many details, such as any type system, are omitted.

1) Procedural Programming: Descriptions of some typical constructs of imperative PLs are shown in Figure 4. Typical control flow constructs, such as conditional statements and loops are given as M³L concepts.

For model checking or for model execution, the language constructs must be given semantics. For example, the behavior of the *ConditionalStatement* can be defined as shown in Figure 5. When evaluated, such a conditional statement will match (become a derived subconcept) of either *IfTrueStmt* or *IfFalseStmt*, depending on which concept a given *Condition* evaluates to. The semantic rule is inherited from the derived base concept, making the statement evaluate to either the "then branch" or the "else branch".

This way of attaching semantics is typical for M³L models; other modeling languages may have different ways of attaching semantics. We will not go into this in detail. However, it is an important part of the PL base models.

2) Functional Programming: Figure 6 outlines base definitions for functional PLs. Note that this model contains definitions that may not apply to all functional PLs, so other APMs exist.

3) Object-Oriented Programming: Only some base definitions for class hierarchies at the instance and class levels are sketched in Figure 7. The complete model is much more

```
Vi is a Variable {
 i is the Name Integer is the Type }
VariDeclaration is a VariableDeclaration {
 Vi is the Variable 0 is the InitialValue}
SomeLoop is a WhileLoop {
 LessThanIntComparison is the Condition {
  Vi is the Left 10 is the Right }
 VariableAssignment is the Body {
  Vi is the Variable
  IntegerSum is the Expression {
   Vi is a Summand 1 is a Summand }}}
```

Figure 8. A sample abstract program.

elaborate, and there are even more variants of PLs than in the other paradigms.

C. Abstract Programs

ADMs can be formulated in the M³L as refinements of APMs. Figure 8 shows an example of imperative code for a loop that increments a variable i from 0 to 9.

D. Abstract Program Transformations

In our experimental setup with the M³L, model transformations can be expressed by relating concepts to each other: one is a refinement or a redefinition of the other. In other modeling languages, the respective model transformation or model evolution facilities are used.

E. Code Generation

The final M2TTs to produce source code are performed on models that combine an ADM with the abstract program for the problem at hand and a CPM that declares concrete PL constructs.

The CPM comes with predefined translation tables that are used to generate code. Such translation tables can be formulated by syntactic rules in the example of the M³L.

For example, rules for language-dependent code generation for two different languages can be such as:

```
Java is a ProgrammingLanguage {
 ConditionalStatement
  |- if ( Condition )
     ThenStatement
     ElseStatement . }
Python is a ProgrammingLanguage {
 ConditionalStatement
  |- if Condition :
     " " ThenStatement
     else:
     " " ElseStatement . }
```

By separating APMs and CPMs, it is possible to generate different code from the same abstract program. In the M³L, concepts can easily be redefined with different syntactic rules in the context of a PL. When generating code in such a PL context, the rules of all language constructs for that PL are used. Variations for language dialects can be handled in sub-contexts where some rules are redefined.

V. Conclusion and Future Work

Model-Driven Software Engineering is receiving a lot of attention for the benefits it brings to software engineering processes. While model-to-model and model-to-text transformations are being researched, in practice the final step of code generation from models is too costly to be applied in many application scenarios.

In this paper, we propose an approach to define code generators for the MDSE toolchain. Code generators consist of executable models that are defined step by step, where each step is characterized by a simple model. In addition, some models are generic and can be shared. If the models that define a code generator are formulated in the same modeling framework as the models for earlier stages of the software engineering process, then models of the application domain and models of the software can be closely related.

The proposed approach allows us to achieve the goals of reduced development costs for code generators and of increased reuse. Using multiple levels of abstraction makes each development step easier and less expensive. Since the most abstract models are generically applicable, they can be reused across applications.

Future work includes experiments with real-world code models before pursuing new research directions. Since many important PLs are hybrid in nature, remaining issues with combined APMs need to be addressed, such as the mismatch between imperative and declarative PLs.

Acknowledgements

The publication of this work was made possible by the NORDAKADEMIE gAG.

References

[1] H.-W. Sehring, S. Bossung, and J. W. Schmidt, "Content Is Capricious: A Case for Dynamic System Generation," Proceedings Advances in Databases and Information Systems, Springer, 2006, pp. 430–445.

[2] H. Mannaert, K. De Cock, and J. Faes, "Exploring the Creation and Added Value of Manufacturing Control Systems for Software Factories," Proceedings Eighteenth International Conference on Software Engineering Advances, ThinkMind, 2023, pp. 14–19.

[3] K. Lano and Q. Xue, "Code generation by example using symbolic machine learning," SN Computer Science, vol. 4, Springer Nature, 2023.

[4] T. Mucci. *What is a code generator?*, Think 2024, [Online] Available from: https://www.ibm.com/think/topics/code-generator. 2024.6.28.

[5] T. E. Shulga, E. A. Ivanov, M. D. Slastihina, and N. S. Vagarina, "Developing a software system for automata-based code generation," Programming and Computer Software, vol. 42, pp. 167—173, 2016.

[6] K. Radek and J. Vladimír, "Incorporating Petri Nets into DEVS Formalism for Precise System Modeling," Proceeding Fourteenth International Conference on Software Engineering Advances, ThinkMind, 2019, pp. 184–189.

[7] Object Management Group. *MOF Model to Text Transformation Language, v1.0*, OMG Document Number formal/2008-01-16, [Online] Available from: https://www.omg.org/spec/MOFM2T/1.0/PDF. 2024.7.4.

[8] M. Harter, "LLM Assisted No-code HMI Development for Safety-Critical Systems," Proceedings Sixteenth International Conference on Advances in Human-oriented and Personalized Mechanisms, Technologies, and Services, ThinkMind, 2023, pp. 8–18.

[9] S. Hajiaghapour and N. Schlueter, "Evaluation of different Systems Engineering Approaches as Solutions to Cross-Lifecycle Traceability Problems in Product Development: A Survey," Proceedings International Conference of Modern Systems Engineering Solutions, ThinkMind, 2023, pp. 7–16.

The Hidden Hazards of Job Hunting: Third-Party Services on Job Search Websites

Esko Vuorinen, Sampsa Rauti, Timi Heino, Henna Lohi, Sammani Rajapaksha, Panu Puhtila
Department of Computing
University of Turku
Turku, Finland
e-mail: {etvuor | sjprau | tdhein | hmlohi | syraja | papuht}@utu.fi

Abstract—**This paper explores third-party services and trackers used on job search websites. We analyze what kind of data on the job search process is sent to these third parties and whether users have a fair possibility to understand what kind of data collection is taking place on the studied websites. Our results show that 87.5% of the studied websites leak data on the user's actions, such as displayed job advertisements, search terms and the intent to apply for a specific position. One job search website could leak data to as many as 9 third parties. Websites run by public sector bodies had significantly less third parties and data leaks, however. While some third parties may be necessary for targeted advertising, it would be important for website maintainers to consider the number of third parties and better inform users about the data protection activities.**

Keywords-Data leaks; third parties; web analytics; job search websites; online privacy.

I. Introduction

More and more often, recruiting and seeking jobs happen online [1][2]. Job search websites have become a tool of choice for internet users looking for vacant jobs [3][4]. With these online platforms, users can now effortlessly hunt for jobs by browsing job openings and submitting applications. However, many job search websites are also businesses trying to make profit. Therefore, website maintainers add third-party web analytics services to these websites to monitor the fulfillment of their business goals and to measure the quality of user experience. Job seekers are now faced with a privacy risk, often unknowingly.

When users navigate on the job search websites, browse through job listings, and show interest in specific positions, their actions are monitored and recorded. While the justification for this is often said to be collecting data for the company that runs the job search website, data is also gathered by the third party that hosts the web analytics service, such as Google. Tracking job search activities secretly undermines users' privacy. This is especially true if users are not transparently informed of the fact that third-party services are deployed on the job search websites. Informing users inadequately of the data processing activities that taking place prevents users from giving proper and genuine consent and making truly informed decisions about their privacy [5].

In this study, we analyze 16 Finnish job search websites by performing a network traffic analysis and study *what kind of personal data concerning the user's job searches they send to third parties*. We also gauge the transparency of the privacy policy documents on these websites and identify dark patterns in their cookie consent banners. Previous research on privacy of job search websites has usually concentrated solely on the data the user willingly inputs on the job search platforms [6][7], and we extend this research by covering third-party tracking. Our paper also provides an up-to-date overview of the privacy of Finnish job search websites.

The rest of the paper is organized as follows. Section II reviews related work. Section III describes the study setting, explains how the dataset was collected, and presents the method. Section IV discusses the results of network traffic analysis, privacy policies and dark patterns. Section V covers implications for users and offers recommendations for web developers. Finally, Section VI concludes the paper.

II. Related Work

Nickel et al. [7] study user trust in e-recruitment, focusing on how perceived privacy affects user trust. They found that an interface that conveyed a high level of privacy also increased trust users place in the web service. Users that trusted the service more also disclosed more sensitive information. It is worth noting that perceived privacy and actual privacy can be very different, especially with third-party services that are invisible to the user. In a similar vein, Wijayanto et al. [6] report that platform credibility and users' awareness have a positive correlation with the willingness to share personal information in an online job portal. While the privacy of job search websites has been discussed by several studies, third parties have not received the attention they deserve. Our study aims to fill this gap.

The privacy risks of including third party analytics in web services have been widely studied [8]–[10]. The dangers of Uniform Resource Locators (URL) and search terms leaking to third parties have also been discussed in the literature [11], and the need for analytics solutions that do not share users' personal data with external parties has been acknowledged [12].

Third-party analytics and trackers have been found to be common privacy challenge in web services covering many critical application areas. The dangers of third parties have been explored for example in health-related websites [13], online pharmacies [14], goverment websites [15], and voting advice applications [16] just to name a few. The current paper presents, to the best of our knowledge, the first study on third-party analytics services on job search websites and the possible implications of such third-party data leaks.

III. Study Setting, Data collection, and Method

In the current study, we examined 16 job search websites. As there appears to be no official list of largest Finnish job search websites, we attempted to choose the most popular and well-known job search websites in Finland, based on Google search results and several sources listing job search services. Therefore, we believe the chosen websites form a representative sample of Finnish job search websites.

The selected services include both public sector websites (Kuntarekry, TE-palvelut, Työmarkkinatori, Valtiolle) and websites run by private companies (Academic Work, Adecco, Atalent, Barona, Biisoni, Duunitori, Eezy, Eilakaisla, Jobly, Manpower, Oikotie, Staffpoint). However, it is not our intention to discuss or criticize the privacy of specific companies or organizations, but rather adress the phenomenon of data leaks from a holistic perspective. Therefore, in the current paper, the websites are referred to by pseudonyms WS1–WS16, assigned in a random order.

Our experiment involved running a short testing sequence on the selected websites. All cookies were consented to upon arriving at the selected websites. First, from the main page, a search for a specific job title was initiated. On the results page, the first job advertisement in the results was chosen and clicked. Finally, on a specific job advertisement page, the "apply for the job" button or link was pressed, indicating an intent to apply for a position.

We recorded the network traffic by employing Google Chrome's Developer Tools (devtools). This set of tools allowed us to examine network activity during the testing sequence. The analyzed network traffic was filtered so that only the web requests going to third parties were inspected. The recorded traffic was also saved as log files for later analysis. From the log files, we extracted any data sent to third parties that could be used to identify the user or contained sensitive contextual information (such as data showing an intention to apply for a job). In other words, personal data items were collected from the network traffic.

In addition to network traffic analysis, we also examined on whether dark patterns – user interface design techniques to deceive users into accepting cookies and consenting to data collection [17] – were present in the cookie consent banners of the analyzed websites. We chose to use the dark pattern definitions of the European Data Protection Board's Cookie Consent Banner Taskforce [18]. We chose to focus on following specific dark patterns, which were the most unambiguous to detect and assess, detailed in the report:

- The "reject cookies" button is not present on the first layer of the cookie banner, making it harder to reject cookies and data collection than to accept them.
- Pre-ticked consent boxes or other predefined choices are used, which is not sufficient for obtaining unambiguous and freely given consent required by the General Data Protection Regulation (GDPR).
- Deceptive use of button colors or contrast is present to psychologically manipulate the user by the deployment of specific colors. For example, the colors are used to unfairly highlight the accept button so that the user is deceived into clicking it.

Finally, we briefly define the term "personal data". In this study, we employ the definition used in the GDPR and the Finnish Office of the Data Protection Ombudsman: personal data refers to "all data related to an identified or identifiable person" [19][20]. Internet Protecol (IP) addresses, accurate location data, and device or user specific identifiers used by third-party analytics services are examples of personal data. It is also important to note that many pieces of data can be used together to identify a person, and therefore, they are also considered as personal data. For instance, when window size is sent to a third-party service, this data item does not identify a specific user alone, but it can be effectively combined with other technical details to profile users.

IV. Results

In this section we look at the results we retrieved from the prior methods.

A. Network Traffic Analysis

The third parties found in the network traffic analysis are shown in Figure 1. The usual technology giants, Google and Meta (Facebook), are the most frequent third parties, appearing on 12 out of 16 studied websites. Although the use of Google Analytics has raised legal concerns in the European Union [21], Google's services are still widely prevalent. The third one on the list is LinkedIn (8 occurrences), a professional networking platform, which is an expected third party on job search websites. It is also noteworthy that TikTok, a Chinese social media platform which has recently raised privacy concerns in western countries [22], is also present with 3 occurrences.

When it comes to leaking contextual data related to searching for a job, we found that there were three notable categories of data leaks:

1) *Job advertisement page.* The URL of the job advertisement the user is viewing leaks to a third party, thus indicating that specific user shows interest in the job opening.
2) *Search term.* The search term user has used with the search function of the website (such as "Siivoaja" – a cleaner in Finnish) leaks to a third party. This often indicates the user is interested in a specific category of jobs. The search term usually leaks as a part of the URL of the search result page listing the job opportunities.
3) *Intent to apply.* The user's intent to apply for a specific position is leaked to a third party. This is probably the most valuable piece of information that a third party can receive from job search websites, because it often indicates the user's strong interest in a job opening. It often also means the user applied for the job, although some users may click the apply button just out of curiosity or otherwise abort the process of applying to a job before completion. From a technical viewpoint, there

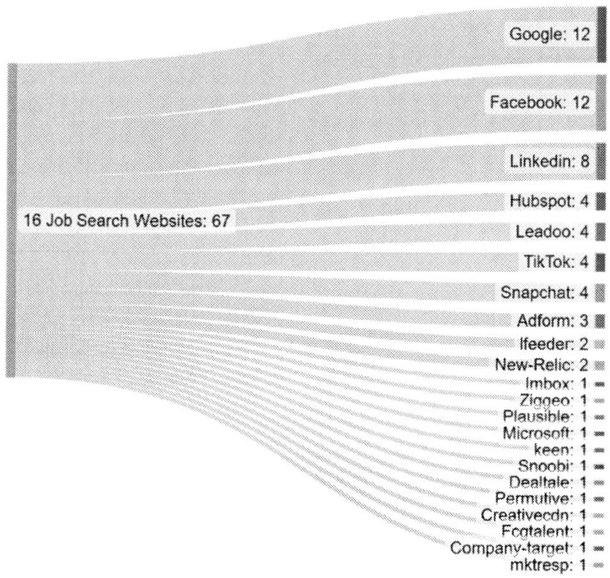

Figure 1. An alluvial diagram showing the third parties on the studied job search websites. Each third party has been counted once per website.

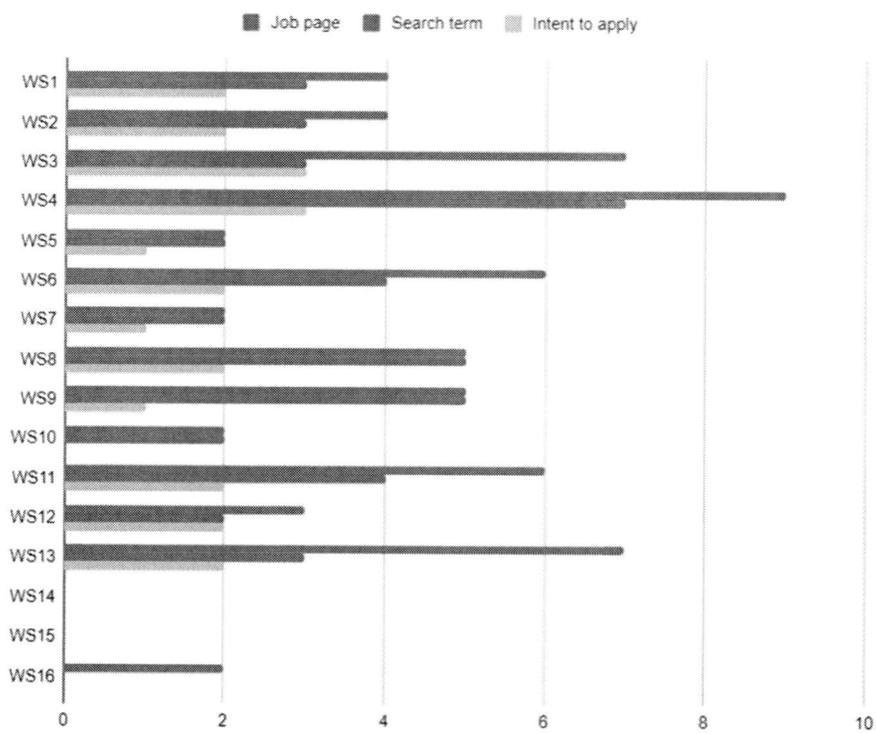

Figure 2. The leaked job search data on different job search websites and the numbers of third parties data was leaked to.

were many ways the information about an intent to apply for a job was leaked, but usually the button click event or form submission along with explicit button or form names reveal that the user has taken an action indicating the start of the job application process.

TABLE I. DARK PATTERNS ON COOKIE BANNERS OF JOB SEARCH WEBSITES.

Website	Asks for consent	Reject button	Pre-ticked boxes	Colors & Contrast
WS1				
WS2				
WS3				
WS4				
WS5				
WS6				
WS7				
WS8				
WS9				
WS10				
WS11				
WS12				
WS13				
WS14				
WS15				
WS16				

Figure 2 shows the leaked job search data on different job search websites, sorted into three categories discussed previously. The diagram displays the number of third parties data was leaked to for each job search website and data category. The leaked job pages are shown in blue, search terms in red and intent to apply for a job in yellow.

It is quite clear that public sector websites – WS10, WS14, WS15, and WS16 – fare better in terms of privacy and third parties. WS14 and WS15 did not appear to have any third-party analytics and did not leak personal data in our experiment. The rest of the websites were maintained by private sector companies, and they had a greater number of data leaks, for example WS4 leaking the viewed job advertisement to 9 third parties, search term to 7 third parties and the intent to apply for a job to 3 third parties. The clearest divide between public and private sector job search websites, however, is in whether they leaked the intent to apply for a job. All of the private sector websites leaked this information, and none of the public sector sites did.

On average, there were 4.2 third-party services receiving personal information per job search website. Private sector websites had 5.3 such services on average, while public sector websites only had 1.0. This clearly shows that, when visiting job search websites, at least the ones run by private companies, one should expect their job search information to be leaked and monetized.

While we have focused on contextual job search data here, it is worth noting that this data would not be valuable without identifying information. Therefore, the data delivered to third parties includes identifying technical details like IP addresses, and unique device and user identifiers, as well as other technical data like screen resolution. For example, every web request contains the device's IP address, an important piece of information when trying to identify a specific user [23][24]. It is also clear that big tech companies like Google and Meta track users with cookies and also usually have the capability to know users' real names and connect them to job seeking data. When this identifying data and contextual data such as the user's intent to apply for a specific job are combined, the user's privacy is compromised.

B. *Privacy Policies and Dark Patterns*

While we gave consent to cookies and data collection in our study setting, it is interesting to ask whether a user can really understand that the information of the job openings they browse, the search terms they use and the job they intend to apply for are all recorded and sent to remote servers hosted by third parties. Can it be said that the user truly consents to this information collection knowingly?

When examining privacy policies, we found that only one privacy policy document mentioned all the third parties that were collecting data on the website (WS6). Also, the fact that data on the job postings user has accessed is collected was also only mentioned in one policy (WS10). The collection of search terms or recording the intent to apply for a specific job opportunity were not mentioned in any of the analyzed privacy policies. Consequently, it can be argued that the transparency of the studied job seeking websites is almost zero and the user cannot genuinely understand what kind of data collection they consent to on these websites.

Table I shows the dark patterns found on cookie banners of the studied job search websites. Positive outcomes are shown in blue, while red describes the fact that a recommended practice has not been followed. All the analyzed websites ask for consent for cookies and data collection, which is a positive result. However, 4/16 websites did not have a reject button on the first layer of the cookie banner, making it more difficult to decline cookies.

Moreover, on 2/16 occasions, cookie banners also contained pre-ticked boxes, trying to get consent without clear and affirmative user action. Three of the cookie banners, marked in black, did not have any tickable boxes. It is worth noting that the GDPR (Recital 32) explicitly addresses the fact that pre-ticked boxes should not be used: "Silence, pre-ticked boxes or inactivity should not [...] constitute consent." This makes pre-ticked boxes essentially illegal [25][26].

Finally, the most common flaw of cookie banners is using misleading colors so that the accept button is portrayed as a prominent and enticing option for users, deceiving them into accepting cookies and data collection. This dark pattern was present in 13/16 cookie consent banners.

V. DISCUSSION

The privacy and confidentiality of job-seeking and applying for a job varies. In Finland, for example, the private sector can keep applications confidential. In the public sector, recruitment is public. Information on applicants can be published and anyone can request to see applications. Still, it is fair to say many applicants applying for a job generally see the application process as confidential. In this section, the implications of the data leaks found in this study are discussed from the viewpoints of users and web developers.

A. *Implication for Users*

Leaking data related to job searches to third parties can have various implications. The use of web analytics and tracking users' activities on job search websites are a cause for privacy concerns. Users' job search queries, job advertisement pages they display, and possibly even their intent to apply for a job are being monitored and collected by third-party services. Most users are probably not even aware that this kind data collecton is taking place [27]. The user's personal data is compromised when their job search activities are secretly monitored. Because the job seeker is often not transparently informed about third-party services being present on the job search website, it is fair to ask whether they can really give proper consent and make truly informed decisions about their privacy is greatly impeded.

Profiling and targeted advertising are another concern [28][29]. Third-party analytics services collect data on job seekers' interests and search history. It is possible to create user profiles using this information, and customize advertisements displayed to the user online based on their preferences. While this is also a positive thing to many users receiving more interesting job advertisements and opportunities, profiling can also limit the job opportunities the user sees on the web. Obviously, profiles and preferences can also be used for many other purposes besides matters related to job-seeking.

Discrimination during the recruitment process is also possible. The personal data collected by third party services could be used to treat job seekers in an unfair manner. A job seeker's job preferences or past job search activities could have an effect on recruitment decisions, if an employer were to obtain this information. An example of this would be a potential employer finding out what kinds of jobs a candidate has viewed or applied for in the past. The employer could use this data to make unjust assessments on how qualified or suitable the candidate is for a job.

A situation where the current employer finds out that the employee is looking for a job elsewhere could also sometimes become a problem. Likewise, in some cases the relatives or friends of an individual learning about what kinds of job openings the individual has been interested in could be highly undesirable. Applying for jobs in controversial companies or politically inclined organizations are some examples of this. Some lines of work, such as front-line service jobs, are also often stigmatized [30]. While it may not be very probable that the data collected by third parties becomes public, an individual's job search preferences can also leak through the advertisements regularly displayed to them, that may also be visible to their employer and the people close to them.

B. *Implication for Developers*

The findings of this study raise some concerns about job-seekers' privacy online. It is obvious that the job search websites need some third parties to do well against their competitors. Targeted advertising on social media is important, as job-seeking often takes place on social media [31][32] and big tech giants also have a great coverage when it comes to advertising on other websites.

Even if we accept some of the third-party tracking taking place on the studied websites, the problem of excessive use of third-party services remains. For instance, having 9 third-party services on one website and leaking personal data to them is simply too much, not to mention this is done without informing users appropriately. Dark patterns on cookie consent banners further exacerbate this problem, as users are surreptitiously coaxed into accepting the data collection.

It is evident that users should be better informed what data related to the job-seeking process is handed over to third parties. Even if job-seeking activities and applying for a job are not usually highly sensitive personal data comparable to data concerning health, for example [9][33], the users should definitely have a possibility to make an informed decision on this data collection. While some users may find targeted advertisements useful and beneficial, there should be a possibility to control them easily.

Considering and choosing the used third-party services carefully is important. The use of each service should be well justified. It is also important to understand where the services send the user's personal data. The network traffic analysis approach discussed in this paper can be used to get a good understanding of what kinds of data the website transmits to external entities. If possible, third-party services should be replaced by locally hosted services such as Matomo [12] that do not leak the users' data to third parties. This way, the privacy-by-design approach is better followed and the user's privacy is respected.

VI. CONCLUSION

It is clear that competition and the drive to fulfill business goals cause the job search websites to use several data-collecting third-party services on their websites. At the same time, the website owners are in many cases responsible for placing the users' privacy in jeopardy without adequately informing them about their data processing activities. We have observed that the visited job advertisements, search terms and intent to apply are regularly leaked to third parties without the user being explicitly informed. At the same time, dark patterns – especially deceptive color choices – are used to persuade users to accept cookies and data collection. Our findings call for increased attention to the use of third parties on job search websites and careful consideration on how these services handle users' personal data.

ACKNOWLEDGMENTS

This research has been funded by Academy of Finland project 327397, IDA – Intimacy in Data-Driven Culture.

References

[1] A. E. Green, Y. Li, D. Owen, and M. De Hoyos, "Inequalities in use of the internet for job search: Similarities and contrasts by economic status in great britain," *Environment and Planning A*, vol. 44, no. 10, pp. 2344–2358, 2012.

[2] A. Gandini and I. Pais, "Social recruiting: Control and surveillance in a digitised job market," *Humans and machines at work: Monitoring, surveillance and automation in contemporary capitalism*, pp. 125–149, 2018.

[3] Jobvite, *Job seeker nation survey 2020: When change is the only constant*, https://www.jobvite.com/lp/2020-job-seeker-nation-report/thank-you/?submissionGuid=dcf1bc49-5922-4c08-9a49-ecf6c01ab09b, 2020.

[4] R. J. Faberman and M. Kudlyak, "What does online job search tell us about the labor market," *Economic perspectives*, vol. 40, no. 1, pp. 1–15, 2016.

[5] S. Breen, K. Ouazzane, and P. Patel, "Gdpr: Is your consent valid?" *Business Information Review*, vol. 37, no. 1, pp. 19–24, 2020.

[6] R. Wijayanto, Y. Ruldeviyani, and I. Sulistyowati, "Analysis factors of personal information sharing in online job portal application," in *AIP Conference Proceedings*, AIP Publishing, vol. 2482, 2023.

[7] J. Nickel and H. Schaumburg, "Electronic privacy, trust and self-disclosure in e-recruitment," in *CHI'04 Extended Abstracts on Human Factors in Computing Systems*, 2004, pp. 1231–1234.

[8] R. D. Gopal, H. Hidaji, R. A. Patterson, E. Rolland, and D. Zhdanov, "How much to share with third parties? user privacy concerns and website dilemmas," *Mis Quarterly*, vol. 42, no. 1, 143–A25, 2018.

[9] M. Huo, M. Bland, and K. Levchenko, "All eyes on me: Inside third party trackers' exfiltration of phi from healthcare providers' online systems," in *Proceedings of the 21st Workshop on Privacy in the Electronic Society*, 2022, pp. 197–211.

[10] C. Utz *et al.*, "Privacy rarely considered: Exploring considerations in the adoption of third-party services by websites," *arXiv preprint arXiv:2203.11387*, 2022.

[11] T. Libert, "Privacy implications of health information seeking on the web," *Communications of the ACM*, vol. 58, no. 3, pp. 68–77, 2015.

[12] D. Quintel and R. Wilson, "Analytics and privacy," *Information Technology and Libraries*, vol. 39, no. 3, 2020.

[13] X. Yu, N. Samarasinghe, M. Mannan, and A. Youssef, "Got sick and tracked: Privacy analysis of hospital websites," in *2022 IEEE European Symposium on Security and Privacy Workshops (EuroS&PW)*, IEEE, 2022, pp. 278–286.

[14] A. R. Zheutlin, J. D. Niforatos, and J. B. Sussman, "Data-tracking among digital pharmacies," *Annals of Pharmacotherapy*, vol. 56, no. 8, pp. 958–962, 2022.

[15] N. Samarasinghe, A. Adhikari, M. Mannan, and A. Youssef, "Et tu, brute? privacy analysis of government websites and mobile apps," in *Proceedings of the ACM Web Conference 2022*, 2022, pp. 564–575.

[16] T. Heino, S. Rauti, S. Laato, R. Carlsson, and V. Leppänen, "Leaky democracy: Third parties in voting advice applications," in *International Conference on Smart Computing and Communication*, Springer, 2024, pp. 351–360.

[17] C. Utz, M. Degeling, S. Fahl, F. Schaub, and T. Holz, "(un) informed consent: Studying gdpr consent notices in the field," in *Proceedings of the 2019 acm sigsac conference on computer and communications security*, 2019, pp. 973–990.

[18] European Data Protection Board's Cookie Consent Banner Taskforce, *Report of the work undertaken by the cookie banner taskforce*, https://edpb.europa.eu/our-work-tools/our-documents/other/report-work-undertaken-cookie-banner-taskforce_en, Accessed: 2024-08-20, 2023.

[19] gdpr.eu, *What is considered personal data under the eu gdpr?* https://gdpr.eu/eu-gdpr-personal-data/, Accessed: 2024-08-20, 2024.

[20] Office of the Data Protection Ombudsman, *What is personal data?* https://tietosuoja.fi/en/what-is-personal-data, Accessed: 2024-08-20, 2024.

[21] S. Winklbauer and R. Horner, "Austrian DPA Decides EU-US Data Transfer through the use of Google Analytics to Be Unlawful," *European Data Protection Law Review*, vol. 8, p. 78, 2022.

[22] S. Patnaik and R. E. Litan, "TikTok shows why social media companies need more regulation," *The Brookings Institution, Policy Brief*, 2023.

[23] V. Mishra *et al.*, "Don't count me out: On the relevance of ip address in the tracking ecosystem," in *Proceedings of The Web Conference 2020*, 2020, pp. 808–815.

[24] T. Heino, R. Carlsson, S. Rauti, and V. Leppänen, "Assessing discrepancies between network traffic and privacy policies of public sector web services," in *Proceedings of the 17th International Conference on Availability, Reliability and Security*, 2022, pp. 1–6.

[25] T. Jakobi and M. von Grafenstein, "What HCI Can Do for (Data Protection) Law—Beyond Design," *Human Factors in Privacy Research*, pp. 115–136, 2023.

[26] P. Puhtila, R. Carlsson, and S. Rauti, "Privacy risks of third-party services on women's shelter websites," in *2023 16th International Conference on Security of Information and Networks (SIN)*, IEEE, 2023, pp. 1–6.

[27] D. Boyd and K. Crawford, "Critical questions for big data: Provocations for a cultural, technological, and scholarly phenomenon," *Information, communication & society*, vol. 15, no. 5, pp. 662–679, 2012.

[28] M. Gjoreski, M. Laporte, and M. Langheinrich, "Toward privacy-aware federated analytics of cohorts for smart mobility," *Frontiers in Computer Science*, vol. 4, p. 891 206, 2022.

[29] S. J. De and A. Imine, "Consent for targeted advertising: The case of facebook," *AI & SOCIETY*, vol. 35, pp. 1055–1064, 2020.

[30] C. Benoit, B. McCarthy, and M. Jansson, "Occupational stigma and mental health: Discrimination and depression among front-line service workers," *Canadian Public Policy*, vol. 41, no. Supplement 2, S61–S69, 2015.

[31] G. Karaoglu, E. Hargittai, and M. H. Nguyen, "Inequality in online job searching in the age of social media," *Information, Communication & Society*, vol. 25, no. 12, pp. 1826–1844, 2022.

[32] C. W. Piercy and S. K. Lee, "A typology of job search sources: Exploring the changing nature of job search networks," *New Media & Society*, vol. 21, no. 6, pp. 1173–1191, 2019.

[33] A. R. Zheutlin, J. D. Niforatos, and J. B. Sussman, "Data-tracking on government, non-profit, and commercial health-related websites," *Journal of general internal medicine*, pp. 1–3, 2021.

On the Object Oriented Petri Nets Model Transformation into Java Programming Language

Radek Kočí

Brno University of Technology, Faculty of Information Technology,
IT4Innovations Centre of Excellence
Bozetechova 2, 612 66 Brno, Czech Republic
email: koci@fit.vut.cz

***Abstract*—Nowadays, high-level languages and approaches to software design and implementation are often used. The main reasons for this are the possibility of faster and more efficient design and more efficient verification of the design produced. To deploy a system created in this way, either a framework can be used to handle the formalism used or the design can be transformed into a programming language or lower-level formalism. In this paper, we focus on the Object Oriented Petri Net (OOPN) formalism and introduce the idea of transforming OOPN models into the Java programming language.**

Keywords*—*Object Oriented Petri Nets; model transformation; Java.

I. INTRODUCTION

The key activities in system development are specification, testing, validation, and analysis (e.g., performance or throughput). Most methodologies use models for system specification, i.e., to define the structure and behavior of the system under development. There are different kinds of models, ranging from low-level formal-based models to purely formal models. Each kind has its advantages and disadvantages. Less formal models, e.g., Unified Modeling Language (UML), allow the basic concepts of a system to be quickly described; on the other hand, they do not allow the correctness or validity of the system to be verified through testing or formal methods – the system must be implemented before it can be tested. More advanced approaches, e.g., Executable UML (ExUML) or Model Driven Architecture (MDA) [1], allow models to be simulated, i.e., provide simulation testing. Purely formal models, e.g., Petri nets, allow formal or simulation approaches to be used for testing, verification, and analysis.

Model and Simulation-Based System Design (MSBD) refers to a set of techniques and tools for developing software systems that are based on formal models and simulation techniques. It aims to improve the efficiency and reliability of development processes, including software system deployment. One way to increase the efficiency and reliability of development processes is to work with high-level languages and models throughout the development process. In traditional system development methodologies, models are typically created in the analysis and design phases and are input in the implementation phase. The system code is implemented manually by reflecting the created models or by transformations. The fundamental problem with model transformations is often the impossibility of a fully automated process and, therefore, the mismatch between models and their implementation. The transformed code needs to be modified manually, and these changes are not fully reflected in the models. However, if we use a formalism that allows us to include parts of the code, the resulting transformed code does not need further modification. The Object Oriented Petri Nets (OOPN) language is one of these formalisms. This paper focuses on transforming models described by the OOPN formalism into the Java programming language.

There are many approaches in the field of code generation. One direction [2]–[4] generates models in the chosen language from UML models, usually from a class diagram. Other work [5] transforms different levels of diagrams. Still, other approaches attempt to transform conceptual models described in, e.g., SysML into simulation models [6]. There are approaches working with simplified variants of UML models (xUML or fUML) from which it is possible to generate the resulting system more precisely [7][8]. However, freely available tools allow only partial output (often, only a skeleton in the chosen language is generated). The approach closest to ours is based on the Network-within-a-Network (NwN) formalism, with which the Renew [9] tool is associated. NwNs combine Petri nets and the Java language, and models are directly translated into Java. Our approach works with Smalltalk, which can be transformed into Java or C++, or we can directly use these languages for inscription. Our goal is to create a more efficient representation of models for deployment on commonly used platforms and languages (Java, C++).

The paper is structured as follows. In Section II, we introduce the basics of the OOPN formalism. Section III describes the basic structure of the OOPN, which is subject to the transformation whose basic principle is described in Section IV. Chapters V and VI discuss the essential element of the transformation, the component, and its runtime in the Java environment.

II. OBJECT ORIENTED PETRI NETS FORMALISM

An OOPN is a set of classes specified by high-level Petri nets [10]. Formally, an OOPN is a triple (Σ, c_0, oid_0) where Σ is the class set, c_0 is the initial class, and oid_0 is the name of the initial object of c_0. A *class* is determined primarily by the object net and the set of method nets. Object nets describe the possible autonomous actions of objects, while method nets describe the reactions of objects to messages sent to them from outside.

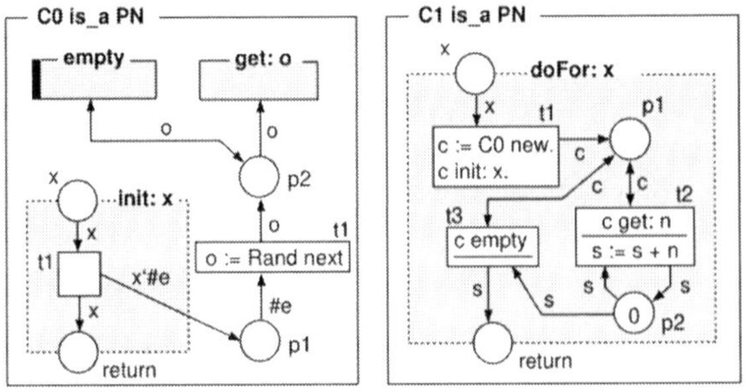

Figure 1. Example of the OOPN model.

An example illustrating the essential elements of the OOPN formalism is shown in Figure 1. Two classes are depicted, *C0* and *C1*. The object net of the class *C0* consists of places *p1* and *p2* and one transition *t1*. The object net of the class *C1* is empty. The class *C0* has a method *init:*, a synchronous port *get:*, and a negative predicate *empty*. The class *C1* has the method *doFor:*. An invocation of the method *doFor:* leads to the random generation of *x* numbers and a return of their sum.

Object nets consist of places and transitions. Each place has an initial marking. Each transition has conditions (i.e., inscribed test arcs), preconditions (i.e., inscribed input arcs), guard, action, and postconditions (i.e., inscribed output arcs). *Method nets* are similar to object nets, but each net has a multiplicity of parameter places and the return place. Method nets can access the places of the corresponding object nets to allow running methods to change object states.

Synchronous ports are special (virtual) transitions that cannot be executed independently but are dynamically joined to some other transitions that activate them from their guards via messaging. Each synchronous port contains a set of conditions, preconditions, and postconditions over the places of the corresponding object nets, a guard, and a set of parameters. Thus, synchronous ports combine the concepts of *transitions* (must satisfy preconditions and guards; when a synchronous port is invoked, postconditions are executed) and *method net* (must be invoked from the guard of another transition). The parameters of an activated synchronous port *s* can be bound to constants or unified with variables defined at the transition level or port that activated the port *s*.

Negative predicates are special variants of synchronous ports. Their semantics are reversed - the calling transition is executable if the negative predicate is not.

III. Basic Structure

Objects create a network of dependencies through their links, which gradually arise and disappear. On the other hand, the internal nets of an object (object net or method nets) have a clearly defined structure that defines actions and the conditions under which actions can be performed. Each net contains transitions and places. Transitions represent actions whose execution is conditioned on both the existence of the corresponding objects at the entry points and the guarding of the transition. The guard defines the conditions imposed on objects entering the transition. If these conditions are not met, the transition cannot be executed (fired). A transition may be evaluated as feasible and executed for different objects available at the entry points satisfying the guard conditions. Thus, a transition can be viewed as a special kind of component that is dynamically duplicated when the transition is executed and terminates after the last transition action is executed. Thus, transitions, or their execution, represent the internal parallelism of the nets.

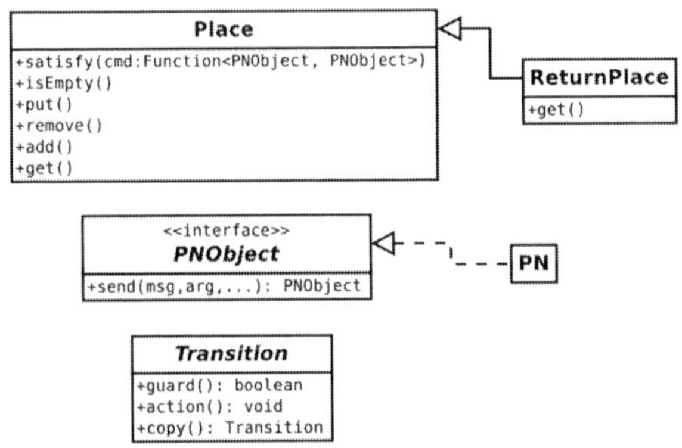

Figure 2. Basic Java classes for OOPN transformation.

Figure 2 shows the basic structure of classes and interfaces required to transform OOPN models into Java. The class Place represents the collection corresponding to a place. In addition to the standard and expected operations for adding, retrieving, and deleting elements, it contains an operation for evaluating a condition placed on the collection's contents. The condition is represented by a function (the Java functional interface Function). When the condition is met, the operation returns an object from the collection that satisfies the condition. The special class ReturnPlace represents the return place of the method nets. It overrides the get method, which is blocking here (it waits for the object to be inserted into the collection, i.e., for the called method to terminate). The meaning of the other elements will be explained in sections IV and V.

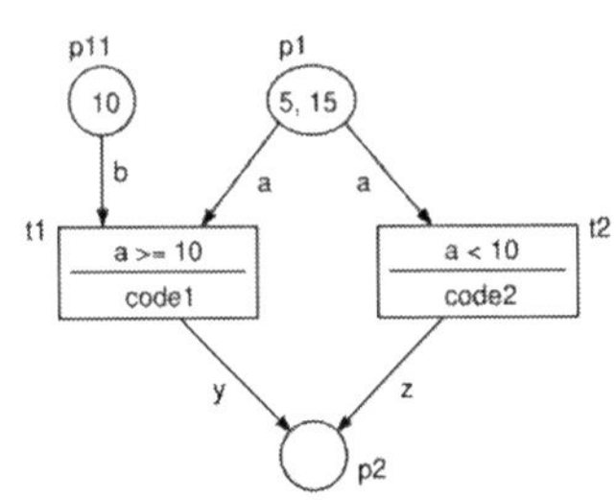

Figure 3. Example: Object net of the class C1.

Consider the simple example in Figure 3. This is an object net of class C1 consisting of two transitions conditioned on places p11 and p1, each transition having in addition its feasibility condition (guard1: a >= 10 and guard2: a < 10). The result of each transition execution is placed at place p2. Thus, executing this net produces a copy of component t1 (for binding a = 5 and b = 10) and a copy of component t2 (for binding a = 15).

IV. Structure Tranformation

A view of the transition as a component can be used to transform the model into a programming language, in this case, Java.

```
public class C1 extends PN {
   protected Place p11;
   protected Place p1;
   protected Place p2;
   public C1() {
      p11 = new Place(this);
      p1 = new Place(this);
      p2 = new Place(this);

      class T_1 extends Transition { ... }
      T_1 t1 = new T_1();
      class T_2 { ... }
      T_2 t1 = new T_2();

      t1.precond(p11, p1);
      t2.precond(p1);
      p1.add(5;
      p1.add(15);
      p11.add(10);
   }
}
```

Figure 4. Translation of the OOPN model of class C1 into Java.

For each transition, a class derived from the Transition class is generated, containing methods to verify the input conditions (guard) and a method containing the actual actions of the transition (action). A place corresponds to an unordered collection of objects from which objects can be read and removed, and new objects can be added. The principle of model translation is shown in Figure 4. It presents a basic structure of Java code based on the model example shown in Figure 3. The following section will describe each aspect of the code.

The class is always derived from the PN class, which provides the primary means for object handling and communication. The object net is represented by a parameterless constructor (if a constructor is used in the model, the generated constructor in Java is adapted to this). The object net's places can be considered attributes (object variables) of the object, and their declarations are therefore placed in the member fields space. They are then initialized in the constructor, i.e., an instance of the Place class representing a type of collection is created. As will be shown later, it is through the place, or by inserting objects into the place, respectively, that invoke the check for satisfiability of transition (component) conditions; the place must pass information about the object through the constructor.

```
public PNObject m(PNObject p1) {
   ...
   Place ret = new ReturnPlace();
   ...
   // Transition::action -> ret.put(result);
   ...
   return ret.get();
}
```

Figure 5. Example of the method translation into Java.

The OOPN object method has a structure similar to an object net. It differs in the following aspects. It can have input parameters that are modeled as places in OOPN. However, since only one object can be inserted into a place when the method is invoked, a variable can be used directly in the generated method. The method can also return an object as its result. In the OOPN model, such a return object is placed into a place named return by performing some transition. Thus, the method must wait before placing the object in the return place. A special ReturnPlace class with a blocking get() method is provided for this purpose. The method will wait until at least one object is inserted into the place. An example of the skeleton of the generated method is shown in Figure 5.

V. Component Definition

Figure 6 shows an example of a component generated by the transition. The component takes the form of a class derived from the Transition class. The implementation of the guard and action methods depends heavily on the model. The binding of variables from input places is reflected in the guard method. In this example, the input places are checked to see if they are empty and if there is an object that satisfies the condition given by the guard of the transition t1. If these conditions are met, the corresponding objects are stored in the component variables, and the guard method is terminated successfully. Following the success, the component's copy is then executed.

Because the OOPN language is typeless, the common type of all variables is the PNObject class, and communication, i.e., sending messages, must be done specially. PNObject is the interface implemented by the PN class and, thus, by all OOPN classes. However, we must consider that models also work with other objects (e.g., primitive Java data types and other Java classes). Therefore, we need wrappers for objects of these classes that implement the PNObject interface to ensure compatibility. The messaging is done via a special protocol (see the call message in Figure 6), ensuring proper redirection to the target object.

VI. Component Execution

The question is how to verify the feasibility of transitions, i.e., the execution of component actions. Repeatedly testing the satisfaction of conditions is obviously inefficient and completely inappropriate. For these purposes, the Observer design pattern can be used. Each place knows the transitions (components) whose feasibility it affects. At the moment of

```
class T_1 extends Transition {
  private PNObject a;
  private PNObject b;
  public boolean guard() {
    // guard1: a >= 10
    if (p11.isEmpty()) return false;
    if (p1.isEmpty()) return false;
    a = p1.satisfy((o) -> o.send(">=", 10));
    if (a == null) return false;
    b = p11.remove();
    p1.remove(a);
    return true;
  }
  public void action() {
    // code1: y = a + b
    PNObject y = a.send("+", b);
    p2.put(y);
  }
  public Transition copy() {
    T_1 t = new T_1();
    t.a = a;
    t.b = b;
    return t;
  }
}
```

Figure 6. Implementation of generated transition t1.

change (it is sufficient to watch for the addition of an object to the place), it notifies all connected components, which verify their state. Access to these collections must be synchronous, as each component is generally expected to run in its thread, and hence, concurrent access may occur. Since verifying the conditions to trigger a transition action (component) must be an atomic operation, a method similar to event-driven programming can be chosen for synchronization. Each object contains a control thread in which the verification of the conditions of all object transitions, i.e., the object net and the method nets, is performed. Since only these nets can access the object places, this will guarantee exclusive access and atomicity of each verification. The control thread is created and started when an instance of the corresponding class is created, and requests for verification of transition feasibility conditions are only processed in its code. The disadvantage of this approach is that the thread exists even after the object is no longer needed and could be removed from memory.

Another approach is to use a monitor that is implicitly available in Java. When invoking condition validation, the object monitor protects the relevant actions within which the places (whether of object net or method nets) are accessed. The monitor object is passed by the constructor when creating an instance of the Place class. A code sample is shown in Figure 7. Each registered transition for which a given place is an input condition is tested for feasibility (called its guard method). If the transition is evaluated as feasible, its action (through the action method) is executed in a separate thread; the executor's service is used via the PNSystem class. Since the component action can be executed simultaneously for different bindings, we need to run the action method of the component copy with

```
void add(PNObject obj) {
  synchronized(monitor) {
    Integer c = content.get(obj);
    c = (c != null) ? c + 1 : 1;
    content.put(obj, c);
    for (Transition t : observers) {
      if (t.guard()) {
        Transition tt = t.copy();
        PNSystem.execute(() -> tt.action());
      }
    }
  }
}
```

Figure 7. The class Place, method add(PNObject).

the current binding in the thread. The copy method is used for this purpose.

VII. Conclusion

This paper aimed to outline the possibilities of transforming the models described by the OOPN formalism into Java. The resulting code does not need to be further modified because the original model allows the use of the code and also objects from the target environment (in our case, Java). The basic principle is quite simple. However, the efficiency of the translated code depends on the analysis of transitions and appropriate optimization techniques. For example, the place corresponding to the input parameter of a method does not need to be generated as a collection because it can contain at most one object. For the same reason, a dependent transition can be executed almost once.

If we include the declaration of [10] types in the OOPN model or automated type derivation, it is possible to replace the generic PNObject type with a specific type in the generated code and thus interact with objects directly by sending messages.

Acknowledgment

This work has been supported by the internal BUT project FIT-S-23-8151.

References

[1] C. Raistrick, P. Francis, J. Wright, C. Carter, and I. Wilkie, *Model Driven Architecture with Executable UML*. Cambridge University Press, 2004.

[2] T. Hussain and G. Frey, "UML-based Development Process for IEC 61499 with Automatic Test-case Generation," in *IEEE Conference on Emerging Technologies and Factory Automation*. IEEE, 2010.

[3] C. A. Garcia, E. X. Castellanos, C. Rosero, and Carlos, "Designing Automation Distributed Systems Based on IEC-61499 and UML," in *5th International Conference in Software Engineering Research and Innovation (CONISOFT)*, 2017, pp. 61–68.

[4] I. A. Batchkova, Y. A. Belev, and D. L. Tzakova, "IEC 61499 Based Control of Cyber-Physical Systems," *Industry 4.0*, vol. 5, no. 1, pp. 10–13, November 2020.

[5] S. Panjaitan and G. Frey, "Functional Design for IEC 61499 Distributed Control Systems using UML Activity Diagrams," in *Proceedings of the 2005 International Conference on Instrumentation, Communications and Information Technology ICICI 2005*, 2005, pp. 64–70.

[6] G. D. Kapos, V. Dalakas, A. Tsadimas, M. Nikolaidou, and D. Anagnostopoulos, "Model-based system engineering using SysML: Deriving executable simulation models with QVT," in *IEEE International Systems Conference Proceedings*, 2014, pp. 531–538.

[7] F. Ciccozzi, "On the automated translational execution of the action language for foundational uml," *Software and Systems Modeling*, vol. 17, no. 4, p. 1311–1337, 2018. doi: 10.1007/s10270-016-0556-7.

[8] E. Seidewitz and J. Tatibouet, "Tool paper: Combining alf and uml in modeling tools â an example with papyrus," in *15th Internation Workshop on OCL and Textual Modeling, MODELS 2015*, pp. 105–119, [retrieved: August, 2024]. [Online]. Available: http://ceur-ws.org/Vol-1512/paper09.pdf

[9] L. Cabac, M. Haustermann, and D. Mosteller, "Renew 2.5 - towards a comprehensive integrated development environment for petri net-based applications," in *Application and Theory of Petri Nets and Concurrency - 37th International Conference, PETRI NETS 2016, Toruń, Poland, June 19-24, 2016. Proceedings*, 2016, pp. 101–112. [Online]. Available: http://dx.doi.org/10.1007/978-3-319-39086-4_7

[10] R. Kočí and V. Janoušek, "The Object Oriented Petri Net Component Model," in *The Tenth International Conference on Software Engineering Advances*. Xpert Publishing Services, 2015, pp. 309–315.

VR-DevOps: Visualizing and Interacting with DevOps Pipelines in Virtual Reality

Roy Oberhauser[0000-0002-7606-8226]
Computer Science Dept.
Aalen University
Aalen, Germany
e-mail: roy.oberhauser@hs-aalen.de

Abstract—**DevOps, with its tools and practices that integrate and automate software development tasks, has become mainstream and offers a host of benefits for modern software development. While the main goal is to foster collaboration with stakeholders, the plethora of platforms and tools, the uniqueness of each pipeline, coupled with a non-uniform display of information (graphical or not), can hinder collaboration and insights, especially for non-developers. Our solution concept VR-DevOps contributes a cross-platform immersive visualization of DevOps pipelines in Virtual Reality (VR). Our prototype realization shows its feasibility, while a case-based evaluation provides insights into its capabilities.**

Keywords – DevOps; virtual reality; visualization; software engineering; continuous integration; continuous delivery; pipelines; automation workflows.

I. Introduction

DevOps [1][2] is a methodology that combines development (Dev) and operations (Ops) with automation to improve the quality and speed of software deliveries. While there is no universally agreed to definition, key principles include Continuous Integration (CI), Continuous Delivery (CD), shared ownership, workflow automation, and rapid feedback. Both the code and tool integration and automation that DevOps addresses has become indispensable to modern software development. It has been reported that 83% of developers surveyed reported being involved in DevOps-related activities [3]. Lately, Security (Sec) has often been included in DevOps, denoted at the stage where it is primarily considered, e.g., DevSecOps [4]. Despite the popularity of DevOps, there are no visualization standards for pipelines; each platform and vendor has their own, and it can thus be difficult for non-developers to grasp - and hence collaborate regarding - the current state of pipeline runs, and the processes involved in software development, testing, and delivery.

Virtual Reality (VR) offers a mediated visual digital environment created and then experienced as telepresence by the perceiver. In contrast to a 2-dimensional (2D) space, VR enables an unlimited immersive space for visualizing and analyzing models and their interrelationships simultaneously in a 3D spatial structure viewable from different perspectives. In their systematic review of the DevOps field, Khan et al. [5] identified a lack of collaboration and communication among stakeholders as the primary critical challenge. Towards addressing this collaboration challenge, our contribution leverages VR towards enabling more intuitive DevOps visualization and interaction capabilities for comprehending and analyzing DevOps pipelines, thereby supporting enhanced collaboration and communication among a larger spectrum of stakeholders. A further challenge is the finding by Giamattei et al. [6] that the landscape for DevOps tools is extremely fragmented, meaning stakeholders access various custom webpages or logs. Hence, a further goal of our solution concept is to unify the visualization and information access across heterogeneous DevOps tools.

An excerpt of our prior VR work related to Software Engineering (SE), DevOps, and workflows: VR-Git [7] and VR-GitCity [8] provide VR-based visualization of Git repositories and version control. VR-SDLC [9] (Software Development LifeCycle) uses VR to visualize lifecycle activities and artefacts in software and systems development. VR-BPMN [10] (Business Process Management Notation) portrays processes in VR. This paper contributes VR-DevOps, a solution concept for visualizing and interacting with heterogenous DevOps pipelines in VR. Our prototype realization shows its feasibility, and a case-based evaluation provides insights into its potential for DevOps pipeline comprehension, analysis, and collaboration.

This paper is organized as follows: the next section discusses related work. Section 3 presents our solution concept. Section 4 describes our realization, followed by an evaluation in Section 5. Finally, a conclusion is drawn.

II. Related Work

For VR-based DevOps-related work, VIAProMa [11] provides a visual immersive analytics framework for project management. DevOpsUseXR is mentioned in the paper as an eXtended Reality (XR) approach for incorporating end users to allow them to directly provide feedback in Mixed Reality (MR) regarding their experience when using a specific MR app. In contrast, our solution concept is independent of the software type being built in the pipeline, and is purely virtual, remaining consistent, app-independent, and focusing on visualizing and collaborating with regard to the DevOps pipeline. The systematic review of DevOps tools by Giamattei et al. [6] does not mention any VR, XR, or MR tools.

Non-VR based DevOps work includes DevOpsML [12], a platform modeling language and conceptual framework for modeling and configuring DevOps engineering processes and platforms. DevOpsUse [13] expands DevOps to collaborate more closely with end users. The authors also state that there is in general a research gap in applying information visualization to software engineering data, and that this needs further investigation. This concurs with our view, as we were not able to find much VR or non-VR work related to DevOps visualization.

III. SOLUTION CONCEPT

Our VR-DevOps solution concept is shown in blue relative to our other VR solutions in Figure 1. VR-DevOps is based on our generalized VR Modeling Framework (VR-MF) (detailed in [10]). VR-MF provides a VR-based domain-independent hypermodeling framework addressing four aspects requiring special attention when modeling in VR: visualization, navigation, interaction, and data retrieval. Our VR-based solutions specific to the SE and Systems Engineering (SysE) areas include: VR-DevOps (the focus of this paper, shown in blue), VR-V&V (Verification and Validation) [14], for visualizing aspects related to quality assurance, VR-TestCoverage [15] for visualizing in VR which tests cover what test target artefacts, VR-Git [7] and VR-GitCity [8] for different ways of visualizing Git repositories in VR. In the Enterprise Architecture (EA) and Business Process (BP) space (EA & BP), we developed VR-EA [16] to support mapping EA models to VR, including both ArchiMate as well as BPMN via VR-BPMN [10]; VR-EAT [17] adds enterprise repository integration (Atlas and IT blueprint integration); VR-EA+TCK [18] adds knowledge and content integration; VR-EvoEA+BP [19] adds EA evolution and Business Process animation; while VR-ProcessMine [20] supports process mining in VR. Since DevOps (or DevSecOps or DevOpsUse) can be viewed as inter-disciplinary, at least for software organizations we view the EA and BP area as potentially applicable for VR-DevOps to support synergies, more holistic insights, and enhanced collaboration across the enterprise and organizational space.

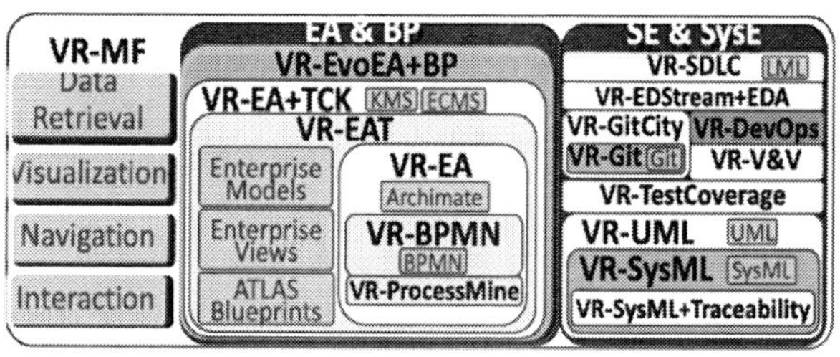

Figure 1. Conceptual map of our various published VR solution concepts with VR-DevOps highlighted in blue.

Work supporting our view that an immersive VR experience can be beneficial for analysis of software-related issues include Müller et al. [21], who compared VR vs. 2D for a software analysis task. They found no significant decrease for VR in comprehension and analysis time. While interaction time was less efficient, VR improved the user experience, was more motivating, less demanding, more inventive/innovative, and more clearly structured.

A. *Visualization in VR*

A horizontal *pipeline hyperplane* represents a pipeline, holding vertical semi-transparent colored boxes called *run planes* (see Figure 2), which are ordered chronologically left to right. A *run plane* represents a pipeline *run*, which is colored based on status (green=success, yellow=in progress, red=error, grey= aborted). Hyperplanes also enable inter-project pipeline differentiation for larger portfolio scenarios involving multiple pipelines. The bottom of each run plane encloses a directed graph of sequential stages (cubes) of the pipeline between a start (black sphere) and an end (black sphere), while vertically stacked smaller cubes linked with lines above each stage show the internal *steps* within a stage. A cube with black borders is used to represent the entire run, and is all that is shown when a run is collapsed (e.g., to reduce visual clutter); on its front various details are depicted (ID, run duration, circular percentage of stages with status). The visualization form remains consistent across DevOps tools.

B. *Navigation in VR*

Two navigation modes are incorporated in our solution: default gliding controls for fly-through VR, while teleporting instantly places the camera at a selected position via a selection on the VR-Tablet. Teleporting is potentially disconcerting, but may reduce the likelihood of VR sickness.

C. *Interaction in VR*

User-element interaction is supported primarily through VR controllers and a *VR-Tablet*. The VR-Tablet is used to provide detailed context-specific element information. It includes a *virtual keyboard* for text entry via laser pointer key selection. On a hyperplane corner, an *anchor sphere*

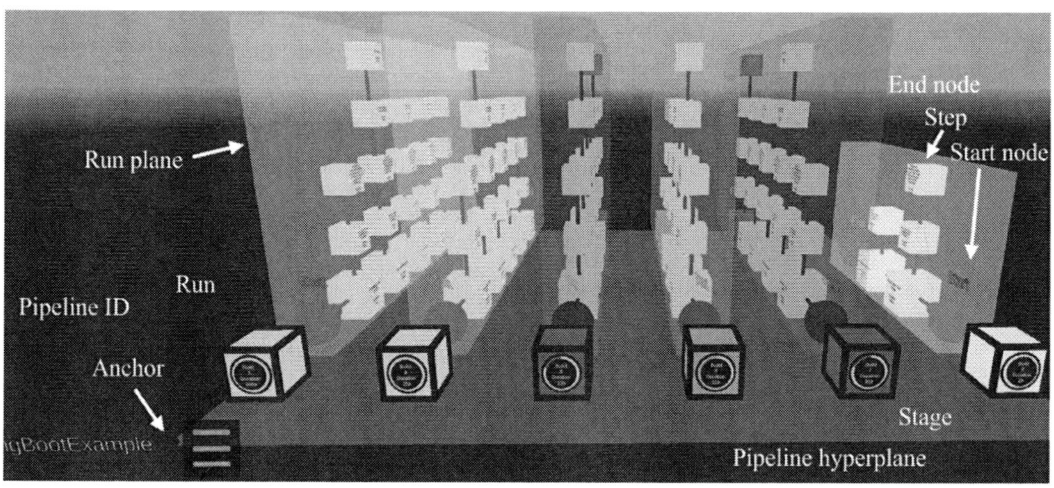

Figure 2. Hyperplane (annotated) of SprintBootExamaple Jenkins pipeline showing vertical colored run planes on a pipeline hyperplane.

affordance (labeled with its pipeline ID) supports moving, hiding (collapsing), or showing (expanding) hyperplanes, as shown in the bottom left of Figure 2.

IV. Realization

In our prototype realization, VR visualization aspects were implemented using Unity. It is supported by a Data Hub implemented in Python that integrates and stores all data in JSON. All integrations with DevOps tools use their Web APIs via our tool-specific Adapters in our Data Hub. The MongoDB Atlas cloud is used for storage (easily switched to a local MongoDB). To demonstrate the tool or platform independence (i.e., heterogeneity) of our solution concept, we chose to integrate with Jenkins, exemplifying a private cloud, as well as SemaphoreCI to exemplify a public cloud tool.

```
    "name": "SpringBootExample",
    "runs": [
      {
        "id": "6",
        "name": "#6",
        "status": "ABORTED",
        "durationMillis": 11910,
        "stages": [
          {
            "id": "8",
            "name": "Declarative: Tool Install",
            "status": "SUCCESS",
            "durationMillis": 160,
            "steps": [
              {
                "id": "9",
                "name": "Use a tool from a predefined Tool Installation",
                "status": "SUCCESS",
                "durationMillis": 47,
                "errorMessage": "",
                "description": [
                  "maven3"
```

Figure 3. Snippet of VR-DevOps common run representation in JSON.

A CD pipeline is an automated expression of the process for preparing software for delivery. A Jenkins pipeline is a set of Jenkins plugins with a set of instructions specified in a text-based Jenkinsfile using Groovy syntax. It can be written in a scripted or declarative syntax, and typically defines the entire build process, including building, testing, and delivery. Concepts involved can include agents (executors), nodes (machines), stages (subset of tasks), and steps (a single task). A SemaphoreCI pipeline is described via a YAML syntax. We created our own common generic JSON format to store pipeline information, see Figure 3. A pipeline instance refers to a run. The refresh rates can be configured for Data Hub state retrieval from Unity and for each Adapter's Web APIs calls.

V. Evaluation

The evaluation of our solution concept is based on the design science method and principles [22], in particular a viable artifact, problem relevance, and design evaluation (utility, quality, efficacy). A scenario-based case study is used (assuming the user may not be a developer): the *Status* scenario focuses on comprehension (run state, number of runs), while the *Analysis* scenario focuses on information retrieval (towards problem identification or resolution). To demonstrate the heterogeneity of the solution, screenshots of runs from Jenkins or SemaphoreCI are interchangeably used.

For Jenkins, the SpringBoot PetClinic example pipeline [23] includes 39 Java files and 1335 Lines of Code (LOC). For SemaphoreCI, the Android App example pipeline [24] includes 13 Kotlin files and 287 LOC. An additional step with an artificial error was inserted into the SpringBoot example for illustration purposes in a second version of the pipeline.

A. Status Scenario

Analogous to a dashboard, a VR-DevOps stakeholder should be able to readily comprehend and assess the current status and state of the various pipeline runs, exemplified for Jenkins in Figure 2 and SemaphoreCI in Figure 10. Each run may execute different steps and stages (e.g., due to an abort or error). Fully collapsed run planes provide a purely high-level overview with relevant info on the black-lined cubes, as in Figure 11. In contrast, every DevOps tool has its own web interface and way of accessing information, illustrated via screenshots of Jenkins in Figure 4 and SemaphoreCI in Figure 5. Retrieval of equivalent status and state details typically requires multiple separate web page requests, thus improving utility and efficacy, especially for increasing pipeline complexity, pipeline versions, and large scale-out of runs.

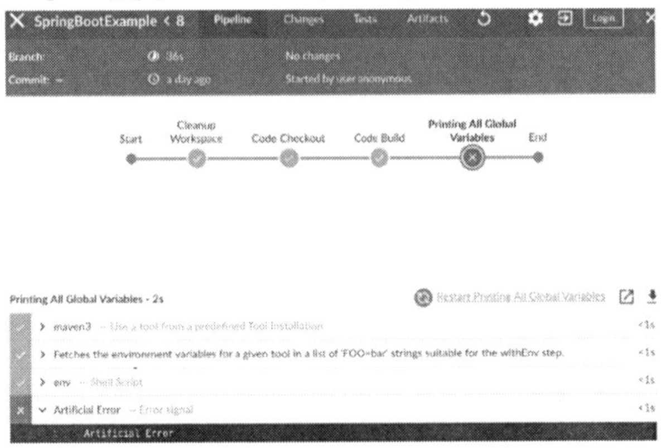

Figure 4. Jenkins tool web screenshot.

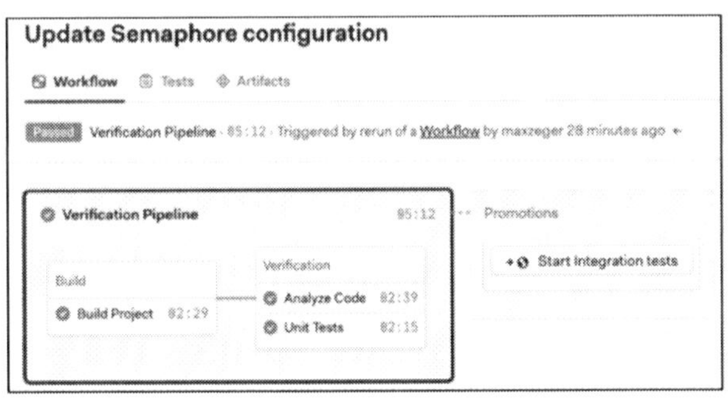

Figure 5. SemaphoreCI tool web screenshot.

B. Analysis Scenario

VR-DevOps supports issue analysis via immersive visual patterns and contrasts, visually revealing differences in pipeline versions and the detailed steps executed shown for the Android App in Figure 6. The contrasts with its YAML (YAML Ain't Markup Language) pipeline definition in Figure

8, which contains many details (difficult for all stakeholders to grasp) but lacks status info, or Figure 5, which provides simplified status, but lacks sufficient overall details. Immersive visual differentiation of runs via perspective and alignment is shown for PetClinic in Figure 7; grasping the pipeline structure from its Groovy file in Figure 9 would be more difficult for non-developers. Visual depiction and differentiation can help support the inclusion of non-tech-savvy stakeholders, improving the speed of assessments and the quality of analysis tasks by including more stakeholders. The VR-Tablet provides additional context-specific metadata and error messages about a block (Figure 12 left), step or stage task instructions (Figure 12 right), or its raw log (Figure 13 left) or pipeline info (Figure 13 right) for developers. This consolidation, in conjunction with visual differentiation, could improve the utility and efficacy of analysis tasks, especially when considering increasing pipeline complexity, pipeline versions, and large scale-out of runs.

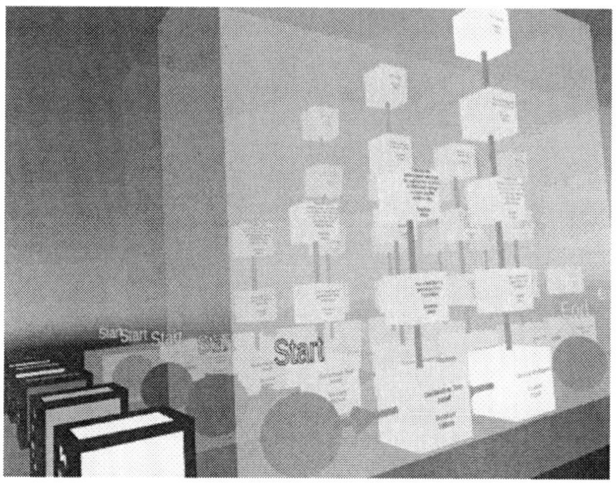

Figure 6. Immersive analysis via visual colored run comparison of stage/step status (for SemaphoreCI pipeline).

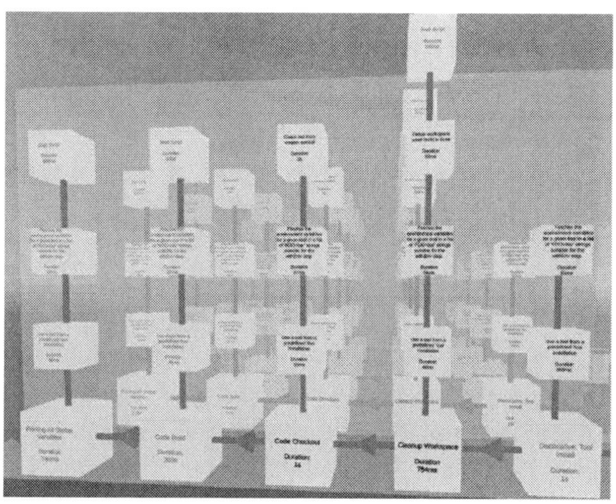

Figure 7. Immersive analysis of pipeline changes via visual alignment of stage/steps (for Jenkins pipeline).

```yaml
version: v1.0
name: Verification Pipeline
agent:
  machine:
    type: e1-standard-2
    os_image: ubuntu2004
  containers:
    - name: main
      image: 'registry.semaphoreci.com/android:29'
global_job_config:
  env_vars:
    - name: ADB_INSTALL_TIMEOUT
      value: '10'
  prologue:
    commands:
      - checkout
      - cache restore gradle-wrapper
      - cache restore gradle-cache
      - cache restore android-build
blocks:
  - name: Build
    task:
      jobs:
        - name: Build Project
          commands:
            - ./gradlew bundleDebug
      epilogue:
        on_pass:
          commands:
            - cache clear
            - cache store gradle-wrapper ~/.gradle/wrapper
            - cache store gradle-cache ~/.gradle/caches
            - cache store android-build ~/.android/build-cache
  - name: Verification
    task:
      jobs:
        - name: Analyze Code
          commands:
            - ./gradlew lint
        - name: Unit Tests
          commands:
            - ./gradlew testDebugUnitTest
      epilogue:
        always:
          commands:
            - artifact push job --expire-in 2w --destination reports/ app/build/reports/
promotions:
  - name: Start Integration tests
    pipeline_file: integration-tests.yml
```

Figure 8. SemaphoreCI Android App pipeline in YAML format

```groovy
pipeline {
    agent any
    tools {
        maven 'maven3'
    }
    options {
        buildDiscarder logRotator(
                    daysToKeepStr: '15',
                    numToKeepStr: '10'
            )
    }
    environment {
        APP_NAME = "DCUBE_APP"
        APP_ENV  = "DEV"
    }
    stages {
        stage('Cleanup Workspace') {
            steps {
                cleanWs()
                sh """
                echo "Cleaned Up Workspace for ${APP_NAME}"
                """
            }
        }
        stage('Code Checkout') {
            steps {
                checkout([
                    $class: 'GitSCM',
                    branches: [[name: '*/main']],
                    userRemoteConfigs: [[url: 'https://github.com/spring-projects/spring-petclinic.git']]
                ])
            }
        }
        stage('Code Build') {
            steps {
                 sh 'mvn install -Dmaven.test.skip=true'
            }
        }
        stage('Printing All Global Variables') {
            steps {
                sh """
                env
                """
                error "Artificial Error"
```

Figure 9. SpringBoot PetClinic Jenkins pipeline in Groovy (snippet)

VI. Conclusion

VR-DevOps provides an immersive solution concept for visualizing, analyzing, and interacting with DevOps pipeline runs in VR. The realization prototype showed its feasibility, and the case-based evaluation showed its potential to support typical scenarios such as status and analysis. The solution concept is DevOps tool-independent, hiding the differences that the fragmented DevOps tool landscape might present to non-tech-savvy stakeholders. It thus provides a way towards broader inclusion of various DevOps stakeholders, and can thus support greater collaboration and communication to address one of the top challenges facing DevOps. Combining VR-DevOps with our other VR solutions, such as VR-Git, VR-GitCity, VR-SDLC, VR-EA, VR-V&V, VR-TestCoverage, etc., can support more holistic DevOps insights.

Future work includes: a VR-native collaboration and annotation capability, additional DevOps tool integrations, and a comprehensive industrial empirical study.

Acknowledgment

The authors would like to thank Maximilian Zeger for his assistance with the design, implementation, and evaluation.

References

[1] C. Ebert, G. Gallardo, J. Hernantes, and N. Serrano, "DevOps," in IEEE Software, vol. 33, no. 3, pp. 94-100, May-June 2016.

[2] L. Bass, I. Weber, and L. Zhu, *DevOps: A Software Architect's Perspective*, Addison-Wesley Professional, 2015.

[3] L. Dodd and B. Noll, "State of CI/CD Report 2024: The Evolution of Software Delivery Performance," SlashData and the Continuous Delivery Foundation, 2024.

[4] GitLab, "A Maturing DevSecOps Landscape," 2021. [Online]. Available from: https://about.gitlab.com/images/developer-survey/gitlab-devsecops-2021-survey-results.pdf 2024.09.12

[5] M. S. Khan, A. W. Khan, F. Khan, M. A. Khan, and T. K. Whangbo, "Critical Challenges to Adopt DevOps Culture in Software Organizations: A Systematic Review," in IEEE Access, vol. 10, pp. 14339-14349, 2022.

[6] L. Giamattei et al. "Monitoring tools for DevOps and microservices: A systematic grey literature review," Journal of Systems and Software, vol. 208, 2024, p.111906.

[7] R. Oberhauser, "VR-Git: Git Repository Visualization and Immersion in Virtual Reality," 17th Int'l Conf. on Software Engineering Advances (ICSEA 2022), IARIA, 2022, pp. 9-14.

[8] R. Oberhauser, "VR-GitCity: Immersively Visualizing Git Repository Evolution Using a City Metaphor in Virtual Reality," International Journal on Advances in Software, 16 (3 & 4), 2023, pp. 141-150.

[9] R. Oberhauser, "VR-SDLC: A Context-Enhanced Life Cycle Visualization of Software-or-Systems Development in Virtual Reality," In: Business Modeling and Software Design (BMSD 2024), LNBIP, vol 523, Springer, Cham, 2024, pp. 112-129, https://doi.org/10.1007/978-3-031-64073-5_8.

[10] R. Oberhauser, C. Pogolski, and A. Matic, "VR-BPMN: Visualizing BPMN models in Virtual Reality," In: Shishkov, B. (ed.) Business Modeling and Software Design (BMSD 2018), LNBIP, vol. 319, Springer, 2018, pp. 83–97, https://doi.org/10.1007/978-3-319-94214-8_6.

[11] B. Hensen and R. Klamma, "VIAProMa: An Agile Project Management Framework for Mixed Reality," In: Augmented Reality, Virtual Reality, and Computer Graphics (AVR 2021), LNCS, vol 12980, Springer, Cham, 2021, pp. 254-272.

[12] A. Colantoni, L. Berardinelli, and M. Wimmer, "DevopsML: Towards modeling devops processes and platforms," In: 23rd ACM/IEEE Int'l Conf. Model Driven Engineering Languages and Systems: Companion Proc., ACM, 2020, pp. 1-10.

[13] I. Koren, "DevOpsUse: A Community-Oriented Methodology for Societal Software Engineering," In: Ernst Denert Award for Software Engineering 2020, Springer, 2022, pp. 143-165.

[14] R. Oberhauser, "VR-V&V: Immersive Verification and Validation Support for Traceability Exemplified with ReqIF, ArchiMate, and Test Coverage," Int'l Journal on Advances in Systems and Measurements, 16 (3 & 4), 2023, pp. 103-115.

[15] R. Oberhauser, "VR-TestCoverage: Test Coverage Visualization and Immersion in Virtual Reality," In: Proc. Fourteenth Int'l Conf. on Advances in System Testing and Validation Lifecycle (VALID 2022), IARIA, 2022, pp. 1-6.

[16] R. Oberhauser and C. Pogolski, "VR-EA: Virtual Reality Visualization of Enterprise Architecture Models with ArchiMate and BPMN," In: Business Modeling and Software Design (BMSD 2019), LNBIP, vol. 356, Springer, Cham, 2019, pp. 170-187, https://doi.org/10.1007/978-3-030-24854-3_11.

[17] R. Oberhauser, P. Sousa, and F. Michel, "VR-EAT: Visualization of Enterprise Architecture Tool Diagrams in Virtual Reality," In: Business Modeling and Software Design (BMSD 2020), LNBIP, vol 391, Springer, 2020, pp. 221-239. https://doi.org/10.1007/978-3-030-52306-0_14.

[18] R. Oberhauser, M. Baehre, and P. Sousa, "VR-EA+TCK: Visualizing Enterprise Architecture, Content, and Knowledge in Virtual Reality," In: Business Modeling and Software Design (BMSD 2022), LNBIP, vol 453, Springer, 2022, pp. 122-140. https://doi.org/10.1007/978-3-031-11510-3_8.

[19] R. Oberhauser, M. Baehre, and P. Sousa, "VR-EvoEA+BP: Using Virtual Reality to Visualize Enterprise Context Dynamics Related to Enterprise Evolution and Business Processes," In: Business Modeling and Software Design (BMSD 2023), LNBIP, vol 483, Springer, 2023, pp. 110-128, https://doi.org/10.1007/978-3-031-36757-1_7.

[20] R. Oberhauser, "VR-ProcessMine: Immersive Process Mining Visualization and Analysis in Virtual Reality," Fourteenth International Conf. on Information, Process, and Knowledge Management (eKNOW 2022), IARIA, 2022, pp. 29-36.

[21] R. Müller, P. Kovacs, J. Schilbach, and D. Zeckzer, "How to master challenges in experimental evaluation of 2D versus 3D software visualizations," In: 2014 IEEE VIS International Workshop on 3Dvis (3Dvis), IEEE, 2014, pp. 33-36.

[22] A.R. Hevner, S.T. March, J. Park, and S. Ram, "Design science in information systems research," MIS Quarterly, 28(1), 2004, pp. 75-105.

[23] B. Wilson. *Jenkins Pipeline Tutorial For Beginners*. [Online]. Available from: https://devopscube.com/jenkins-pipeline-as-code/ 2024.09.12

[24] GitHub. *Semaphore demo CI/CD pipeline for Android*. [Online]. Available from: https://github.com/semaphoreci-demos/semaphore-demo-android/ 2024.09.12

Figure 10. VR-DevOps run status for a set of SemaphoreCI pipeline runs showing expanded step details and an aborted process in grey on the far right.

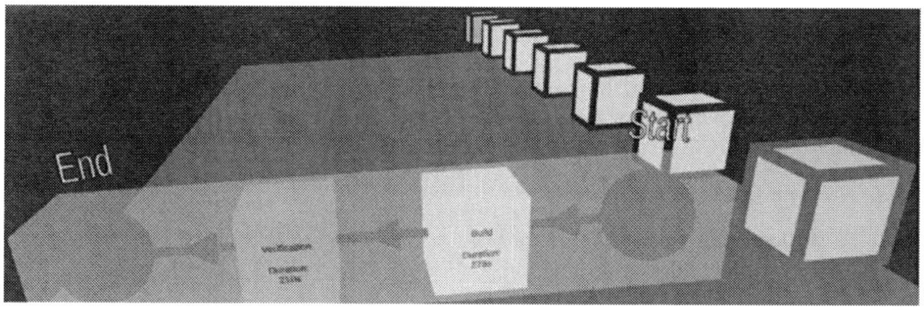

Figure 11. Collapsed SemaphoreCI runs on a pipeline hyperplane with stages expanded (and steps collapsed) for a selected run.

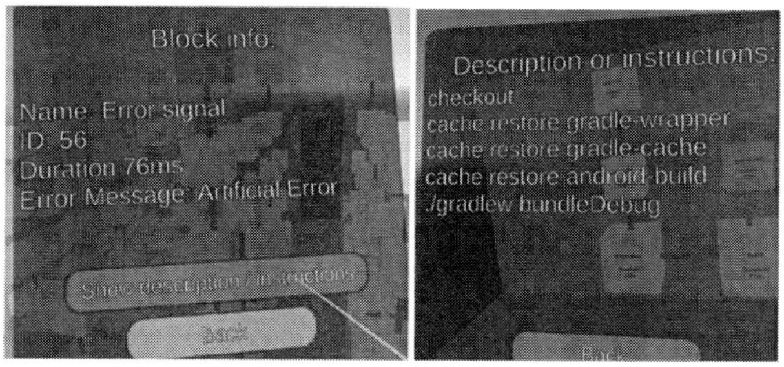

Figure 12. VR-Tablet shows contextual element details: metadata (left) and instructions/description (right).

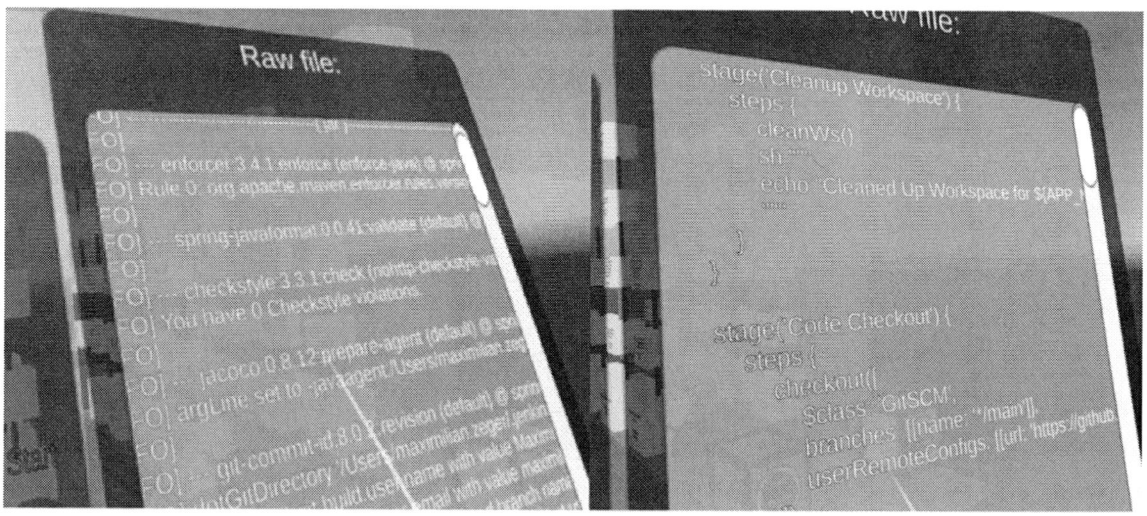

Figure 13. VR-Tablet offers raw file access to log (left) and pipeline (right).

International Academy, Research, and Industry Association (IARIA)
412 Derby Way
Wilmington, DE 19810

ISBN 979-8-3313-0653-3

CURRAN ASSOCIATES INC.
proceedings.com

9 798331 306533

Nineteenth International Conference on Autonomic and Autonomous Systems (ICAS 2023)

Held at InfoSys 2023

Barcelona, Spain
13-17 March 2023

IARIA